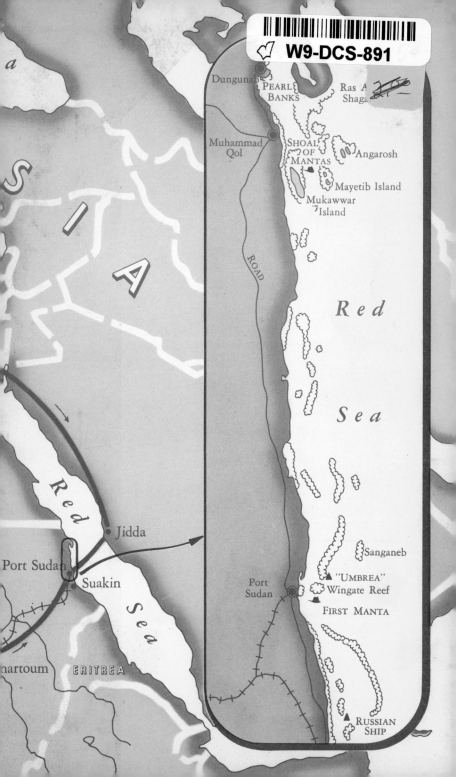

Dungunab

PEARL BANKS

Ras A Shaga

Muhammad Qol

SHOAL OF MANTAS

Angarosh

Mayetib Island

Mukawwar Island

ROAD

Red

Sea

a

S I A

Red

Jidda

Port Sudan

Suakin

Sea

hartoum

ERITREA

Port Sudan

Sanganeb

"UMBREA" Wingate Reef

FIRST MANTA

RUSSIAN SHIP

MANTA

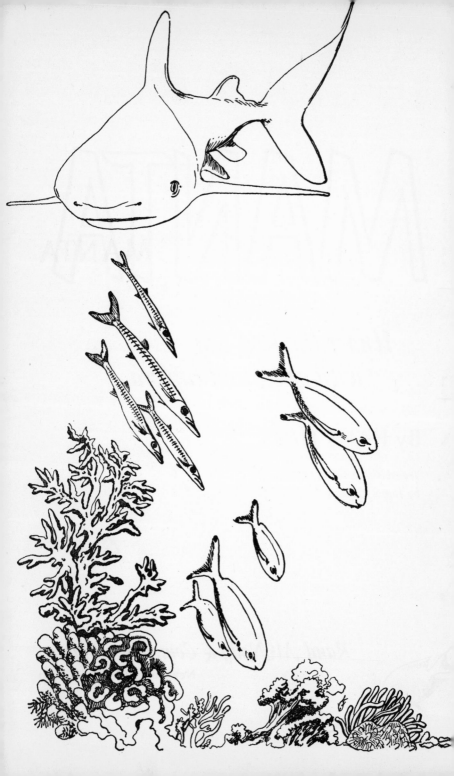

MANTA

Under the Red Sea
with spear and camera

By HANS HASS

*Translated from the German
by James Cleugh*

Rand McNally & Company – Chicago
New York • San Francisco

First Printing, May, 1953
Second Printing, July, 1953

CONTENTS

LIST OF PHOTOGRAPHS

48–49   At the foot of a reef I looked up. Ruby-red fish moved up and down the wall.

A big tropical jellyfish, the medusa, drifted toward me. Strange oscillating formations—the open shells of mussels —peeped out between the coral.

80–81   Mahmud, whose face is tattooed in keeping with the native custom.
Mahmud, O Sheik, and I explored the sea around Port Sudan in this rakish, fifteen-foot felucca.

I glided down to the *Umbrea* where corals had already grown into flowerlike shapes.
The railings running about the deck were festooned with bushy coral clusters.

A butterfly fish hovered about the windlass of the sunken ship.

The broken, rotted ladder led to the interior of the sunken vessel.
At the bottom of the hold I found the dreaded cargo of munitions.

96–97   On our way to Suakin Bill's car is held up by a herd of camels.
The nomadic tribesmen wore their bristled hair combed up on end.

The silhouette of Suakin, the ghostly dead city, came into view.
The blank and empty façades of the ancient palaces stood out against the sky.

Mustapha baited a three-hook line and cast it down a thousand feet.
One of Mustapha's catch. The great depth from which it was brought up caused its eyes to bulge.

I came across beds of thistle coral, with jagged points, and fluffy Alcyonaria.
Three gleaming gold dots, apparently motionless, faced the current.

If I moved, butterfly fish (*top*) and angelfish (*bottom*) came gliding up in panic.

Beside the wall of a coral reef, about fifty-five feet down, bulged the gigantic head of a brain coral.
In the shallow water above the plateau of the reef panther rays were performing a round dance of courtship.

Disappointed not to have gotten the shot I wanted, I sighed. . . . . Then the female ray made straight for me.
I found grottoes that ran far below the solid block of reef for more than 150 feet.

The female panther ray was right up to me now, just turning and gliding off sideways over the corals.
The dreaded firefish has pectoral fins which resemble a peacock's tail.

The next day following a heavy rain I visited the West African Village of Port Sudan.
A Negro woman allowed me to photograph her face.

The shoal, with its hundreds of inquisitive eyes, approached me.

144–45 *"Girsch kabir!"* the men shouted excitedly. I looked where they were pointing and saw two fins, racing about in a playful fashion.
I was overboard in a trice.

Any fish may be greedily seized by the dangerous tentacles of the giant sea anemone. . . . .
But these pomacentrids are allowed to hide in its maw.

176–77 I looked up and saw a phalanx of threatening eyes directed upon me.
Camera failure was a constant bogy.

I saw a great gray shape come gliding through the circle of barracudas. A shark!
Each time I surfaced, it seemed as though I had returned from another world.

I stopped beneath a high, jutting cliff of coral. With its protective wall at my back, I lay in wait for Red Sea sharks.

From the boat Bill watched me through the waterscope.
I glided down into the depths in search of fish.

192–93 Above the sea the sun was preparing to sink behind the clouds.
Below the sea an enormous butterfly—a manta ray—swam round me in a wide arc.

The keepers at the lonely lighthouse at Sanganeb gave us a friendly welcome.
In grottoes burrowed under the banks of sheer coral at Sanganeb I discovered "puffo."

240–41 I stealthily swam up to the right side of the deformed manta and photographed the pilot fish.
Then, to get an even better view of these pilot fish, I made my way above his back, between the flippers.

256–57 Like fantastic monstrous birds the mantas swung through the water, with regular upward (*top*) and downward (*bottom*) beats of their flippers.

I watched pyramid crabs build spired heaps of sand.
A young hammerhead shark.

The only signs that remained of Dr. Crossland's former Institute were posts and pearl-mussel shells.
Every morning this old beggar showed me the hideous skin disease that affected his feet.

Christmastime on the desert! And I ride a camel.

264–65 The childlike old fellow in the center was said to have been one of the crew of the Russian ship.
Under the Red Sea the ship had now turned into a coral reef.

How fast do coral formations build up? Here is the rail of the *Umbrea*.
And here is the rail of the Russian ship.

The deck of the Russian ship was overgrown with coral.
Amidst all this beauty a ferocious-looking spiny-rayed perch guarded the interior.

Five times a day the Mohammedan bows his head toward Mecca.

MANTA

DEPARTURE FOR
THE UNKNOWN

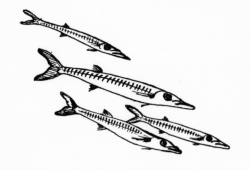

DEPARTURE FOR THE UNKNOWN

THE IDEA of traveling alone to the Red Sea came to me on a warm summer evening in 1949 while I was strolling through a park in Vienna, feeling extremely dissatisfied both with myself and my circumstances. My research vessel, the *Sea Devil,* had been carried off as legitimate booty at the end of the war; practically all its equipment had been lost; the value of my bank account had depreciated. My plan to undertake an up-to-date submarine expedition into tropical seas had vanished like a glittering drop of water in the sand.

I paced on, thinking of the past, gone beyond recall. Then, suddenly, the thought struck me: after all, why dwell on past misfortunes? Surely it would be far better to make a complete break and then, somehow or other, a fresh start.

Yes, a fresh start! Obviously, in my position I couldn't dream of fitting out a new expedition—that was out of the question. But why should I not take up my diving work again on my own initiative, without assistants, and go off somewhere to look for coral reefs built up from unexplored depths of the sea? I could get on with my research even if I were alone; I could hunt, make my observations, and take submarine photographs.

Then, with my new material I could give lectures again, write articles and books, and thus lay a fresh foundation for bigger enterprises. I should run more risks, to be sure, but then I should be quite independent. I could let myself in for hardships and not have to listen to any complaints but my own; and I could stake my life, if I chose, without having to account for my actions to anyone.

Equipment? In a month or two I could easily get what I needed again. I didn't want to travel in luxury, and once I reached my destination, I'd manage somehow. And if my work went well, I should soon find backers again to help me fit out a bigger expedition. Afterward a film could be made, and if it were a success, it would provide the money for a new research vessel. Now I had a road to follow and a goal to achieve which would be worth every effort I could make. The first time it had taken me only five years to get hold of a research vessel of my own. The second time I might succeed even sooner!

I worked out a plan of action, tackling first the problems likely to take the longest to solve. The objective of my journey was already clear: I meant to make for the Red Sea. Port Sudan would be the best jumping-off place. Ten years before I had found out all I could about the locality; at that time, just before the outbreak of war, it hadn't been possible to get a visa for the territories under British protection, but the situation had now improved. I called at the offices of the British Consul in Vienna and asked to see one of the gentlemen on duty.

I laid on the desk before him, by way of a visiting card, my book about the expedition to the Caribbean Sea.*

"Very interesting indeed," said he, after glancing at a few of the illustrations. "How on earth did you manage to deal with those sharks?"

"You just don't let them see you're frightened," I answered. "The brutes are as sharp as needles at spotting anything like that."

"Really? Is that all?"

"Yes. If you come up against sharks under water you have to swim straight at them, as if you were going to attack them. Sharks aren't used to that sort of attitude, for no other fish will go for a shark; so they think you've got the whip hand over them, and off they go."

"But suppose one of them stays? Doesn't that happen sometimes."

"Oh, yes. Then you've got to yell at him for all you're worth."

"Yell? What, under water?"

"Yes. You can puff air into the water and make a kind of squealing noise, and you can easily prove this by trying it in your bath. Sharks are very sensitive to pressure changes in the water, so they turn tail and make off."

The official shook his head in disbelief, and then took me to see his chief. The latter agreed to help me. He advised me to send my application for a Sudan tourist's visa direct to Khartoum and said he would recommend its issuance. I obtained further recommendations from the Vienna Museum of Natural History and the Ministry of Education, and promptly dispatched my petition.

*Diving to Adventure.

I didn't get on so well with the shipping lines. Most of the steamers going through the Red Sea are bound for South Africa, India, or Australia; and as there is a big demand for passage to such places, they are not much interested in a traveler only going as far as Port Sudan. I was told that all berths were booked for the next six months.

I then applied to the representative of a Swedish airline who turned out to be an enthusiastic angler. He promised to try to get his company in Stockholm to grant me a reduction in the fare. I heard from him only ten days later. They would be prepared to meet my wishes, but the airline could only allow me to take a certain quantity of luggage free. I figured it out and reluctantly came to the conclusion that I should only be able to take sixty-six pounds of caustic soda for my respirator. That would be just enough for twenty-five diving descents of an hour each. I should certainly have to make good use of them!

I got some valuable information about the peculiarities of the Red Sea and its inhabitants from the works of Klunzinger, the Austrian naturalist who between 1862 and 1875 had acted as a quarantine medical officer at Quseir, on the Red Sea. I should have been glad, too, to take up the study of Arabic, but there was not enough time for that. Some experts on the country, whom I went to see, advised against the purpose I had in mind. I should certainly be devoured by sharks, I was told, the very first day; there was only one shark-hunting station in the whole world, they said, that regularly worked at a profit and that was at Massaua on the Red Sea. I was told that a passenger who fell overboard at Port Sudan had been torn to pieces by sharks under the very eyes of his companions before he could be rescued. A professor, who had himself explored the coast, described a savage fight to the death he had witnessed between two sharks, in shallow water.

I was also warned against the heat, said to be unendurable by a European. The coast of the Red Sea is the hottest region in the entire world. The sea water there, at its surface, reaches temperatures up to 104° F. Nevertheless, I shouldn't be arriving at the very hottest season of the year; and besides, I had always hitherto felt half frozen while diving. As soon as I had word from Khartoum—I found I had only been granted a visa for fourteen days, but was informed that I could assume it would be extended as soon as I arrived at my destination—I settled the date of my departure, by air, for November 14.

That morning I awoke at six o'clock. It was still quite dark outside. When I looked out the window, I saw that rain was falling in torrents. I dressed quickly; and at half-past six, when the general dealer on the corner opened her shop, I was her first customer. My luggage was almost all packed, but I needed a suitable cardboard box for my rubber bag with the sixty-six pounds of caustic soda. Frau Finsterl, the shopkeeper, at once got me what I wanted. One of her sugar boxes was such a perfect size that it might have been manufactured solely for my benefit.

A few doors further on I bought a ball of stout string and came home again, dripping. Meanwhile Lotte, my secretary, had arrived. She helped me finish packing, and we checked over carefully, once more, our lists of what had to be taken. And a lot of mail still had to be answered. At ten o'clock everything was ready, and we sent for a taxi in order

23

to get to the airport in time to have the boxes and packages sealed by Customs.

On the way we stopped at Kurt's. He was a technical-school student who had undertaken to supply me with a waterproof cover for my miniature camera. I found him in his room, which looked like a battlefield. He was sitting on the floor, covered with grease, his hair in complete disorder.

Instead of greeting me, he simply said, "It's vanished! I've looked everywhere, but it's simply vanished!"

"What's vanished?"

"Oh, that stupid screw! One of those tiny little ones that secure the lens ring gear. It suddenly fell out of my hand and now it's simply vanished."

We crawled round the room together. At last I found the little screw in his wastepaper basket. A few goldfish, swimming in a bowl placed high up out of the way on a trunk, regarded our antics with astonishment. We quickly adjusted the screw and the camera was ready. Lotte, who was waiting down below in the taxi, had already started sounding the horn. The bus for the airdrome left at two and before then everything had to be ready.

We drove to Customs. Luggage dispatch, we were told, would be dealt with in the vast NO. 10 shed. Unluckily, we hit on a functionary there who did not seem to think that anything existed in the world except what was on his lists. My diving gear and submarine cameras did not figure in them. They were articles which had not been anticipated by Customs authorities. The man searched his schedules anxiously. He was obviously worried.

"I've really no business here at all," I told him impatiently. "As I'm leaving the country, I don't have to pay duty on any of my stuff. I only just want you to seal my luggage so that I don't get into trouble on the way through Rome and Cairo."

But the man was now thoroughly immersed in the problem of his Customs lists and couldn't be induced to part with it. He fetched more books and hunted through their pages. A dispatch clerk who was looking on came to our rescue. His point was that my submarine cameras were, after all, only cameras, and cameras—photographic film being made of celluloid—came under the heading "Celluloid." As for my diving gear, that consisted of rubber and brass. This helpful hint gave me the key to the other fellow's honest heart. My cameras were duly listed under "Celluloid" and the diving gear under "Rubber and Brass." Formalities being thus complied with, the Customs inspector wished me all success in my business.

It was still raining hard. We had had a dry period for weeks before this day, and heaven was now making up for its neglected duties. While the taxi drove us round and round Vienna, I settled the rest of what had to be done. Then I got home, had lunch, and arrived punctually at two o'clock in the airline offices. I watched, rather uneasily, my extensive luggage being reweighed and the charge for excess weight calculated.

Lotte kept me company; she wanted to see me off from the airdrome. We waited until half-past four; then at last we were bundled into the bus.

"I still simply can't believe that tonight I shall be sleeping in Rome and tomorrow night in Cairo," I said, as we left the gray outer suburbs of Vienna behind.

Lotte gave a deep sigh. "I envy you! I'd go with you like

a shot if I could! I sometimes get quite angry because I'm not a man!"

"But if you were you wouldn't have those lovely curls any more."

"Don't you believe me? Perhaps I'll prove to you one of these days that a woman may be just as good a choice for an expedition as a man. I wouldn't be at all frightened to go diving with you in the Red Sea!" Her green eyes sparkled. It looked as though she meant what she said.

"At a distance it all seems very fine and romantic," I said. "But if you had to face heat and vermin, the coral skinning you, and every minor scratch festering—I'm not sure whether you'd like that too. Now would you?"

"That's when I should begin to enjoy it!" Lotte had gotten quite excited by this time.

"I should be quite indifferent to all that," she went on. "And if, after this present voyage of yours, you really do set out on a bigger expedition, you ought to take my proposal into serious consideration. A woman can be as tough as a man, if not more so. And a woman can mend and cook and keep everything in order. And a woman can get even more out of the authorities than a man can. She's more economical, too, because she doesn't let herself be swindled so easily when she buys anything!"

The brakes of the bus squealed and we pulled up abruptly. A police car had driven up and was blocking the way. Our driver got out and talked to the police officer. Then we turned round and drove back to the airline offices.

The aircraft had not taken off from Prague owing to the heavy rain. We were to return to the offices at seven the next morning.

I didn't know what to do with myself and went to a theater. At night I tossed, sleepless, in my bed. My room had been cleaned and thus cleared of all traces of my prior occupancy. I felt a stranger there. I had been concentrating inwardly on staying the night in Rome. I had a vision of innumerable sandwiches as I dozed. That was right, the Austrian Embassy in Rome was to give a Press Tea tomorrow. If I could only get there in time!

Punctually at seven o'clock I turned up at the airline offices again. Lotte also came along, as before, to accompany me to the airdrome. It was still raining and the aircraft was apparently still in Prague. However, we were told to be on hand for the next few hours, so we settled ourselves in some uncomfortable chairs.

"You probably won't see it till you get to Cairo now," Lotte said, handing me a copy of an Austrian illustrated paper which had just come out. There was a large photograph of her on the front page. She was shown emerging from the water. Pushed up over her forehead was the circular mask poised on her blond hair like a small modern Paris hat. She was carrying, slung around her neck, my submarine camera!

"Look inside," Lotte said eagerly.

On an inner page of the magazine there was a series of pictures entitled "Expedition into the Viennese Arctic."

She had taken the photographs at the bottom of a quiet tributary of the Danube, at depths of eighteen to twenty-four feet. They were astonishingly clear and sharp in outline. She had photographed forests of weed that looked like a jungle in Borneo; silver sprays of fish spawn hung from the treetops. There was also, by way of still life, an old shoe, half-buried in the mud. Finally came two excellent pictures of large pike, and others of tench, carp, and other water fauna.

"Did you really take these photographs?"

"Yes."

"When did you do that?"

"Two weeks ago, that Thursday you were away."

"But surely it must have been as cold as ice?"

"Yes. Exactly 55°. But that's just the reason the water was so beautifully clear; the small weeds had died off and all the dirt had settled. So don't you agree that if I can dive and take photographs in cold water, I can do it as well in warm?"

That was a dangerous question. I thought it wiser not to commit myself in the matter.

"Tell me, when on earth did I give you permission to take the camera?"

Lotte's eyes grew large and innocent. "You never did. But the end justifies the means!"

We waited for the plane till midday; then the officials gave us an hour off for a meal. It was positively painful to go along the streets. I met acquaintances, one after the other, who all believed I was already in Cairo. The correspondent on one of the papers had made his job easy by writing up my departure in a most touching manner without ever leaving his desk. He couldn't have foreseen, of course, that the aircraft wouldn't leave on schedule.

At two o'clock we again boarded the bus and this time reached the airfield, where the luggage was checked, passports stamped, exchange currency verified and entered on the passport. Then we sat down in the canteen and time began to hang heavy again.

At six o'clock the radio representative declared that he couldn't wait any longer. He had come with the recording car and wanted to take a farewell message for "Today's Echo."

"We're going to broadcast at seven," he explained. "Let's get out there in front of the hangar and you can say a few words. We'll dub in propeller noises from stock afterward."

"And suppose we don't get away after all, again?" I asked, laughing.

But there was no more need to worry now. The plane was already in, and the officer in charge was only waiting for one more weather report, then we should be off. So we asked those present to come out onto the airfield, and it was against a background of general leave-taking that I spoke into the microphone, explaining the object of my journey.

The recording car drove off. A half-hour later we were informed that the plane would not start until early the following morning. I heard my own farewell message in the restaurant where I was having dinner. The propeller sound effects were really very impressive.

Next morning, at the airdrome, there were no more formalities to be gone through. The passengers boarded the aircraft and a few minutes later we were spiraling up through gray blankets of cloud into skies of sunny blue. The plane was only about half-full. The stewardess was a little Dutch girl with a snub nose. When she noticed that I was turning the screw of the yellow disk over the lens of my Leica, she came tripping along the aisle to my seat.

"I'm so sorry, but taking photographs from aircraft is not allowed."

"Oh, why not? I only want to photograph these beautiful clouds."

"Sorry. But that's the rule."

I made my apologies gracefully, the stewardess smiled sweetly and returned to her station. The next time her back was to me, when she was engaged in conversation with another passenger, I took out my camera again. She hadn't mentioned what would happen if I managed to take pictures without her seeing me.

In a short time we could see the Alps. The snow-covered peaks, looking as though carved from lump sugar, soared out of the soft, fluffy blanket of white cloud. Then the clouds began to thin out, and we saw the endless blue of the Adriatic glittering below us. We had a bird's-eye view of Venice, resembling a golden leaf floating in the sea. Florence was covered by a bluish awning of mist, like a cheese-plate cover. We flew over a lake. Then we did a figure eight over the Vatican, and we landed on the Ciampino airfield—a bare two hours after taking off from Vienna.

It was a good deal warmer here than in Vienna. The sky was a cloudless blue. I entered the Customs shed only just in time to stop the Italian official from cutting off my valuable seals with his pocketknife.

"I'm flying on to Cairo this evening," I explained to him. "This luggage is in transit."

He shook his head. "I'm very sorry, but I'm afraid I must open it all the same. We've no facilities here for storing transit luggage under Customs seal."

Other people came up to us and joined in the discussion. The little Dutch stewardess took my side. I was digging out some underwater pictures when another official appeared, who announced that he, too, was an enthusiastic underwater hunter. He said I positively must come to Ischia, where a mysterious fish exists that creeps up into the vineyards at night, has a good meal there, and then rolls back down into the sea, like a ball. There was now no more question of cutting away the Customs leads, but the bus had to wait a good five minutes for me before our discussion as to whether the fish might or might not be a seal came to an end.

As soon as I got into Rome, I called up the Embassy. My telegram canceling the arrangements had unfortunately arrived too late, and sixty journalists had turned up for the reception. However, plenty of sandwiches and vermouth had been brought in for the occasion, so the disappointment was not overwhelming.

My time was my own until the evening, so I strolled about the city at my leisure. My plane was coming from New York and was several hours late. At last it arrived. It was a considerably larger airliner, and the passengers were less friendly than on the Swedish craft. All the seats save one were taken; I was put next to a fat, smelly man who was bound for Calcutta and evidently did not mean to wash until he got there. I turned the air from the ventilator full onto myself and was glad to fall asleep.

When I awoke, the plane had landed. Most of the passengers had already gotten out. It was still pitch-dark. We were in Athens. We were conducted, like a drowsy herd of cattle, through the cool night air to the airline-office building, where a cup of coffee had been prepared for each passenger.

After a half-hour we went on again. When I awoke for the second time, it could not have been much later. Dawn was now breaking and we were flying over flat, dun-colored country, probably the Peloponnesian coast. I expected to catch sight of the sea. But in vain. The country below us was extraordinarily flat, without a single tree or the least sign of vegetation visible. The earth broke in irregular waves and was intersected in many places, like the dried-up sand of an estuary, by irregular fissures.

Suddenly I understood. We had passed the Mediterranean long ago—I was looking at the desert! We should be landing on the airfield at Cairo any moment now.

This realization came to me so suddenly that I got palpitations. I felt like a man in a railway station restaurant serenely ordering a meal and then suddenly discovering that he has miscalculated the time by an hour and that the whistle is already sounding for the departure of his train.

I had pictured the African continent bobbing up in front of us and gradually coming nearer; but now, all of a sudden, here we were. There was a jolt or two, then the plane came to a halt. An Egyptian wearing a red fez entered the aircraft and collected our passports. I hurriedly seized my goods and chattels and followed the others into the open air, onto the sands of the desert.

Shrill cries in French and Arabic rang through the air. There was no sign of a city anywhere. Only a mixture of sand and clay as far as the eye could see, except for the modern buildings of the airport and a sky of dazzling clarity overhead. The sun was just rising over the distant dunes. The first rays that reached us were already noticeably warm.

We were taken into a hall where some twenty officials were busy behind a long table. The first was consulting a large register containing the names of all persons whose ar-

Seven years had passed since my last sea-diving operations. Now I was preparing to begin the adventure afresh, without assistants.

Lotte, my beautiful young secretary, is also an accomplished underwater diver. She was part of the crew I brought back to Port Sudan for the second exploration of the Red Sea coral reefs.

My equipment includes the respirator (*upper left*), oxygen cylinders, submarine cameras, fins, mask, light gauge, film-changing bag, and harpoon barbs. The bag in the center contains enough caustic soda for only twenty-five descents of an hour each.

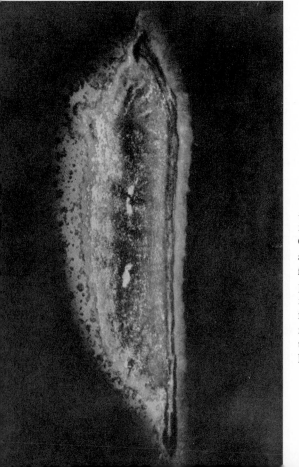

As the airplane that carried me from Athens approached Cairo, I photographed the pyramids. On the way to Jidda we flew across the Red Sea and photographed one of the coral reefs. On one side where the fall of the precipice was abrupt, bottomless depths of water lay right against the sharply outlined edge.

rival would not be welcomed by Egypt; the second collected passports and handed them on to the third; the fourth distributed forms; the fifth filled them out; the sixth received the quarantine fee of five piasters; the seventh changed money for those who did not possess five piasters in Egyptian currency; and so on. The officials continued to gossip, laugh, and change places the whole time: business was done here in an atmosphere of great hilarity.

Hoping to bypass this confusion I sent in my name to the Chief Surveyor of Customs. Three weeks before my arrival an Egyptian paper had published an article about my forthcoming expedition, and with an eye to the future I had had a copy sent me. I presented this paper to the man as proof of my identity.

To my amazement he asked me for news of a lady living at Langwedel near Hanover. She was a relative of his, for it seemed that his cousin had married a German woman, and it was some time since he had heard from her. I hastened to assure him that I would gladly look into the matter. Then I laid my request before him.

"No, no, you'll have no difficulties at all," explained the man obligingly. "You have arrived with a tourist's visa, and we give tourists all possible consideration. Just take all your luggage straight to your hotel and don't bother about it."

That was not quite what I wanted.

"That's very good of you," I said, "but I should prefer to store it with Customs as transit luggage."

"No, no. Once you've got the things with you in the hotel, you can look after them yourself; they'll be all the safer then." He wrote his name and telephone number on the newspaper for me and then handed it back to me with a friendly smile. I need only call him up before I went on with my journey, and he would then see to it that my luggage would get through Customs again without difficulty.

I wasn't quite satisfied with this arrangement. Experience on previous journeys had often proved to me how careful one had to be with friendly officials. The next time you turn up there's someone else there who gets annoyed with his predecessor and is all the more strict for that reason. In this case, however, I need not have worried. The man kept his word, and later on, when I got to know the East better, I realized that he had been perfectly straightforward with me.

On the other hand, the package of caustic soda which I had booked to go by air, caused unexpected trouble. So as not to lose sight of it, I hadn't addressed it direct to Port Sudan, but only as far as Cairo, whence I intended to send it on. Under existing regulations it now had to be imported into Egypt. For this purpose a number of ratifications were required, which, I was assured, would take at least three weeks to obtain. And after that the consignment would have to be exported from Egypt again and that would take at least another three weeks.

My Customs friend couldn't help me in this affair. So, as soon as I got to my hotel, I called up the Austrian Embassy, which at once agreed to intervene on my behalf. All the same, this problem took up all my time during my two days' stay.

I was accompanied on my dreary round from one office to another by an Egyptian film distributor who put himself at my disposal as intermediary and interpreter. During a particularly wearisome interview I saw him getting steadily more and more anxious and continually looking at the clock. He told me afterward that his wife was expecting a baby. We dashed off to his house in a taxi, and there he was informed that all was well and he was the father of a boy.

He danced and jumped about in his delight. "We'll have to celebrate this!" he cried. "It really won't do for you to see nothing of Cairo except its officials!"

That evening he took me around to all the resorts where stomach dancers worth looking at were to be found. He knew them all by their first names, and as they all seemed to want to get a part in one of his films, we never lacked exotic girls at our table wherever we went. Many of them were exceptionally pretty, and the rhythmic contortions they produced to the sound of monotonous flute music were astonishing. It looked as though a rabbit had somehow got into the dancer's stomach and was trying desperately to find a way out.

Next morning we resumed our struggle with the authorities. Finally the Minister of Commerce himself had to be tackled; he released the consignment at once and I relaxed again. But I was a bit previous, for on the very evening I was due to leave, two more wholly unexpected snags turned up. In the first place the small aircraft, which only flew to Port Sudan once a week, had to carry spare parts for another plane which had made a forced landing in the desert; so there was no room for my extensive luggage. In the second place the agent explained to me, long after I had booked my passage and made all the necessary arrangements, that the plane would call at Jidda and that accordingly a transit visa for Saudi Arabia would be necessary. Without such a visa the aircraft couldn't take me.

"And where do I get it?" I asked.

"At the Saudi Arabian Consulate. But it closed long ago."

"Well, what am I to do, then?"

"You can't do anything. All we can do is to book you for next week's plane. You can't go without a transit visa. If you did, it would cause a lot of bother."

"How long does the plane stop in Jidda, then?"

"Ten or twenty minutes."

"There's nothing to be done, then?"

"No, nothing."

It was not until I was about to give up my whole plan that the man suddenly remembered that if I paid twice the fee and all the costs involved, he could cable the visa to Jidda. Grinding my teeth, I agreed to do all that was necessary. And finally, enough room was found, after all, for me to take all my luggage.

We took off at midnight. I had left my overcoat at the office of the Secretary to the Legation at the Embassy and was going to regret it bitterly in the course of the night. The chill of the upper atmosphere drove into this ramshackle aircraft from all sides. Wrapped in a thin blanket and shivering with cold, I wondered what the following day, when I arrived in the hottest place in the world, was going to be like.

My position had been consolidated to an important extent. While I was having my visa entered on my passport in the Cairo office of the British representative for the Sudan, the latter had given me a personal message for Bill Clark, the Commissioner at Port Sudan. He was the keenest fisherman along the whole coast, I was told, and would certainly be of assistance to me, if he didn't happen to be away just then. He would probably actually come with me himself.

As senior British Governmental official he was all-powerful in the town.

"He's an old school friend of mine. Give him my best regards and when you get back, come and see me and let me know how he's getting on," the representative had told me.

I fell into a deep, shivery sort of sleep. When I awoke, the first light of dawn was already clearing the sky. We were flying over the Red Sea. Far below I could see a dark blue sheet of water, intersected by irregular lines, and fading into impenetrable mists in every direction. The mists gradually changed color in the gathering red of the breaking day.

I racked my brain, wondering what those white patterns in the sea might mean. As they did not move, it occurred to me that they were possibly jellyfish, drifting in enormous masses below the surface. Accumulations of this kind are familiar in many places at certain seasons of the year. Later on, as the day grew brighter, I gradually became cognizant of the altitude at which we were flying. No doubt it was the foam of big waves that I could see down there. Looked at from a height of six thousand feet, of course they didn't seem to move.

Then the first coral reefs broke the surface. They were the first true reefs I had ever seen in my life, for in the Caribbean Sea and in Hawaii I had only gotten to know the fringes of coral growing along steep coastal gradients.

In this area the reefs were massive walls rising straight out of the sea, far away from the coast. Many were in the form of long barriers or tangled chains; others were quite small and lay like little reddish mushrooms across the blue-black abyss, rising out of the depths of the sea like slender towers. The long reefs had slanting declivities on one side;

I could distinguish there, on the clear, sandy bottom, tall, isolated, sticklike growths of coral, which faded into impenetrable blue as depths increased. On the other side the fall of the precipice was so abrupt that midnight-blue, bottomless depths of water lay right against the sharply outlined edge of the reef.

We flew over a circular atoll, too; it was lying beneath the waves like a reddish garland of flowers. I kept a sharp lookout to see if I could spot the shape of a shark or some other big sea beast anywhere, but we were flying too high for that. I was filled with a sense of joyous expectation, mingled with a delicious thrill at the prospect of my forthcoming encounter with the unknown—the Red Sea.

The Arabian coast grew more and more clearly delineated before us. A flat strip of desert edged the sea; further off, quite a distance away, the silhouettes of a graduated series of mountain ranges were outlined, as though with a sharp-pointed pencil, against the sky. The coast was also bordered by reefs, which presented a vertical wall to the sea. A few fishing vessels lying at anchor there made one realize the majestic bulk of the reefs; the ships looked no bigger than flies at the bottom of a wall.

We flew in a circle over Jidda Harbor, where a number of bigger vessels were moored, and then over the city itself, glistening like white marble as it rose out of the brown desert. When the door of the aircraft was opened, a rush of air, as if from a blast furnace, burst in upon us. The heat was so palpable that I felt like pushing it away with my hands. Something dense and sultry spread over one's chest, lungs, and all the rest of one's body. It was like a troublesome fur overcoat which hampers all one's movements and which, when walking, one has the definite feeling of pushing against.

"And this is the climate I've got to serve in," sighed a young Englishman who was flying to Eritrea to carry out his military duties somewhere on the Ethiopian frontier.

"How long will you have to stay?" I inquired politely.

"Nine months," was the far from enthusiastic reply.

In the shadow of a primitive building we were served two big jugs of ice-cold grapefruit juice, then off we went again, up into the cooler airs of heaven. Barely two hours later we had crossed the Red Sea for the second time and the Sudanese coast came in sight. It was just like the Arabian. Here, too, a wide margin of desert was hemmed in by distant mountain ranges; but the latter were considerably higher.

A striking feature of the landscape was the number of deep lagoons that licked their way into the desert from the sea, like long, thin tongues, and finally broadened out into the shape of a four-leaf clover. The origin of these natural harbors, called *mersa* by the Arabs, is a hitherto still unsolved problem. Beside a particularly large specimen of "clover leaf" I caught sight of the chessboard pattern of a city laid out on modern lines.

I excitedly examined the reefs in the sea opposite. Below them the fate of my enterprise would be decided! We had come to our destination. We were over Port Sudan!

THE FIRST DAY

THE FIRST DAY

WE FLEW over a flat strip of desert, covered with isolated clumps of bushes—it was Bill Clark's golf course, I learned later—and landed on a piece of waste ground. Passport and luggage-checking took place here in a tiny hut. A very lanky Negro, black as ebony, who wore a uniform, buried himself in my papers.

"What about your yellow fever inoculation certificate?" he inquired, in excellent English.

"I'm afraid it's not possible, for the moment, to be inoculated against yellow fever in Vienna."

"Why not?"

"Because there isn't any vaccine. Inoculation is only possible in Switzerland, and I couldn't get to Switzerland to have it done."

The man nodded and contented himself with my inoculation certificates for smallpox, typhoid and paratyphoid fever, and cholera. Here in the coastal region there was little or no yellow fever. It would only be if I wanted to travel into the interior of the Sudan that I should have to get myself inoculated.

On the other hand, my luggage, which was opened here for the first time, aroused more interest than I felt I wanted. Three Sudanese, ferociously tattooed on the cheeks, examined with startled expressions in their big round eyes the submarine cameras and diving gear. Here, too, Customs lists were dug out, so I thought I had better leave my whole equipment in the hands of the Customs. I only had the case containing my ordinary things passed and took it away with me. A taxi belonging to the airline was waiting for me. I told the driver, tattooed like the rest, to take me to the Red Sea Hotel, which had been recommended to me in Cairo as being the only possible one.

We drove for a while through the desert, with its dusty clumps of bushes, and then reached the poverty-stricken hovels on the outskirts of Port Sudan. They were frame structures of thin, narrow boards, unplaned and overlaid with the tin from gasoline drums hammered flat; this being rusty, they presented an extremely wretched appearance. They were in striking contrast to the proud bearing of the natives who inhabited them.

The men, clothed in white and with perfect physiques, wore their bristly hair ingeniously parted; their sharply outlined features and less fleshy lips clearly distinguished them from the Sudanese Negroes, whose skin is also much darker. The women were swathed from the tops of their heads to their bare feet in purple, bright red, or black fabrics, with only their eyes showing through a narrow slit in the material. These natives were Bejas, nomads of the desert who had come to settle in the country. Some of the men carried a stick across the back of the neck, holding it in the crooks of their elbows. Out in the desert the Bejas still carry the old-fashioned, long sword; in the city, where alcohol is served, the English have forbidden this weapon.

An immense number of screaming children dashed about the dusty streets. We forced our way, tooting loudly, among caravans of camels, heavy trucks, and teams of donkeys. Hideous vultures looked down on us from a high steel scaffolding. The streets gradually widened, and instead of rusty-tin huts we came upon blocks of stone buildings with shady arcades erected against their frontages. Here stood the shops and stalls of merchants. Next we drove past a park and some very pretty villas in the European style. We stopped at a large stone building standing apart from the rest. To left and right of the steps ascending to the entrance, tables stood, dotted about on two terraces. This was the Red Sea Hotel.

An attendant carried my bag into the lobby, where the atmosphere of dignified repose prevailed, characteristic of all hotels run by the British in the tropics. Under the framed picture of a fish once caught in the vicinity—probably constituting a record—an Englishman in white shorts, sitting in a basket chair, briefly glanced at me from behind his newspaper. A big map of the Red Sea and some more pictures of captured fish decorated the other walls of the spacious room, furnished with well-upholstered furniture.

In the background loomed the entrance to a bar. Near the desk of the reception clerk there was a glass case containing silverware, carved ivories, and other souvenirs intended for sale. Close by, in a frame, the latest assortment of Sudanese stamps was displayed, with and without special markings. So dignified was the atmosphere in this room that at a later date when a drunken sailor started talking at the top of his voice here and generally kicking up a row, none of the attendants made a move and not one of the residents took the slightest notice. After a while the police came and took the man away. The gentlemen absorbed in their newspapers had not once interrupted their reading.

The Negro reception clerk opened his large register with a weary gesture. Yes, there was a room free. It was ROOM 25 on the second floor. The charge was eighty piasters a day, including breakfast, or 130 piasters with full board. He reached for a bell and after a time another attendant answered it. The latter picked up my bag and led me, with majestic step, to the second floor.

The room was not large, but it seemed to be airy. Just inside the door stood a large screen, to permit the door to be left open, even at night, without anyone being able to see into the room. The attendant put down my bag, turned on the ventilator—a gigantic propeller in the center of the ceiling which at once started to revolve and distribute a cooling draft—and then waited for his tip.

I washed hurriedly and put on a clean shirt. Armed with my book and a written recommendation I re-entered the taxi. The driver had in my absence joined some other Negroes who were seated some distance away under a shabby looking palm, gossiping. He rose wearily. I requested him to take me to the Commissioner.

Three turnings further on we pulled up in front of a large, solidly built villa, with an extremely well-kept garden surrounding it. I saw a big American car standing under the stone archway of the drive. With some hesitation I entered the garden and then walked in through the front door, which stood wide open. Surely this couldn't be the government building. But, of course, it was Sunday! And only nine o'clock in the morning! This must be Bill Clark's private residence!

In the hall there was nothing to be seen or heard of either staff or owner. To the right and left of the staircase, at the back, cavalry banners were suspended. In a cloakroom to my left I saw fishing tackle and a bag of golf clubs. Next door was a spacious drawing room, where I noticed a remarkable number of silk-shaded floor lamps placed all around the room. Fine Persian carpets and deep, softly upholstered settees indicated a householder who knew how to make himself comfortable. A painstaking arrangement of flowers on a glass table in the center of the room signified a manservant devoted to his master.

"Hello!" I heard someone call out behind me.

In a doorway across the hall an athletic-looking man had appeared, his deeply tanned countenance contrasting strikingly with his wavy gray hair. This man had broad, strongly marked cheekbones and smiling blue eyes. His only garments were shorts and an open, short-sleeved polo shirt, which he wore like a loose jacket.

"Hello," I stammered back. "I'm looking for the Commissioner."

"I'm the Commissioner," he answered. "Come along in. I'm just having breakfast."

We entered a large dining room, where the Commissioner was taking his meal, alone, at a long, polished table. A few French paintings were hanging on the walls and also the portrait of a Sudanese soldier. An open door at the opposite end of the room led to a library, which looked rather untidy. There, too, several big floor lamps, with shades of white silk, outlined the room.

We sat down. The Commissioner turned his head abruptly and called out in a loud voice, "Achmed!"

As no answer came, he repeated the name twice more, giving, each time, a still louder emphasis to the syllable "—med" and drawing it out still longer. At last a distant "*Tai!*" resounded.

Silently a manservant entered. My immediate impression was of black and white patches, all over. First came his bare black feet; then a long, white nightshirt, from which his black hands emerged on each side; and his black head at the top, the head being surmounted by a gigantic turban of dazzling whiteness. There was also a white streak in the middle of the head—his teeth, which he showed me in amicable greeting.

The Commissioner gave him some instructions in Arabic; he was evidently being ordered to lay a second place. We had coffee, a fish swimming in oil, toast, butter, and grilled bacon. As soon as the Commissioner saw the first illustrations in my book—he had merely glanced at my written recommendations—he pushed back his chair and began to question me avidly. He was particularly interested in information about sharks. That one could swim up to a shark holding a camera, he simply wouldn't believe.

"They must have been very friendly sharks you met over there," he said. "Your activities wouldn't do for us here at all. I've been in this place twenty years, but I've never yet heard of anyone proposing to take to the water round the reefs out there. I'm afraid you're going to have some unpleasant surprises. But I'll be delighted to help you in any way I can."

A street scene in Port Sudan. Below are Achmed, the houseboy and Achmed, the chauffeur; and Bill Clark, the Commissioner.

The corals glimmered like a bright, multitinted wreath of flowers,
and many spread out into wide overhanging platelike formations.

At the foot of a reef I looked up. Ruby-red fish moved up and down the wall, streaks of sunlight shooting among them like arrows.

A big tropical jellyfish, the medusa, colored in opalescent shades of blue, drifted toward me. With pulsating rhythmical movements its bell-like shape dragged an enormous quantity of long stinging threads.

Strange oscillating formations were peeping out between the rocks —the open shells of mussels which were bedded among the corals. So sensitive were they to water vibration, they closed as I approached from a distance of thirty feet.

He invited me to come and stay with him for the time being. He was a bachelor and I could see how he relished anything in the way of a change.

"We can go out this very afternoon if you like," he said. "I've ordered the government motorboat for three o'clock, as I want to go fishing; you might just as well come with me and try your luck."

When I told him about the difficulties I had had with my luggage, he put on his slippers and we drove together in his car to Customs. To right and left of the radiator of the car fluttered the pennants of England and Egypt. Wherever we went the Negro policemen saluted and stood at attention. My luggage had been brought from the airfield to the Customs Building, situated on the other side of the many branches of the harbor. As it was Sunday, the formalities, in spite of the presence of high rank, took some time. I had to pay down a deposit for the cameras; I obtained my diving gear and the rest of my equipment without payment in return for a promise that they would be re-exported. Here, too, trouble started over the caustic soda. But by this time the Commissioner had lost patience. He stamped his foot angrily —and the caustic soda was released.

At the dockside I saw the first bright-colored coral fishes. There was a little coral even in the shallow water, but it was poorly developed, for corals only thrive in clean, freely moving waters. As soon as the formalities were over we drove back and Achmed showed me my room. It was on the second floor and opened onto a spacious stone balcony bedecked with flowers; a private bathroom went with it. I found to my satisfaction that the bathroom could be easily darkened; I could develop my films here without trouble.

Lunch was taken as informally as breakfast. We had soup, then fried fish, followed by mutton with potatoes and beans; then came chocolate ice cream and finally coffee. As I was to discover later, this menu hardly ever varied.

"I eat quite simply here," the Commissioner explained. "But if you've ever been to England, you won't be surprised at that."

"And by the way," he added. "It's a bore for me to have to keep on giving you that 'Doctor' title of yours. I suggest that I just call you Hans and you call me Bill. That's quite usual out here."

He was going to have a short rest until three o'clock. Meanwhile I went off to my room to unpack and get ready for our excursion. A stock for the harpoon was a problem; in order to lessen the luggage weight, I had only brought the iron shaft to which the detachable barb is fitted. Where could I get hold of a suitable stock on a Sunday, in this place? I called Achmed and told him what I needed. He disappeared and came back at once with a domestic broom and a semicylindrical molding which had formerly been part of a huge picture frame. As I didn't want to deprive the household of its implements, I chose the molding. But the wood was so hard that I had to shave one end down for a half-hour before I could fit it into the tin casing of the iron shaft.

"Hello!" Bill was ready and waiting for me in the hall.

"Hello!" I ran downstairs, with my spear and fins in hand, to the car.

The police launch was already waiting for us in the harbor. It was a somewhat worm-eaten affair with a decrepit engine, run by two Negroes of martial bearing. They wore short white trousers and seamen's caps. After some refractory snortings and spittings the engine got going, and we moved toward the open sea.

No fewer than four large freighters were moored at the quay in the harbor. The railroad brought cotton, ground-nuts, ivory, and other animal and vegetable products from the interior of the country for transshipment. The deck of one of the vessels was crammed chock-full of cattle which stood penned close together uttering piteous lowings. One after another of the beasts was caught up by a big crane and swung through the air to dry land. At the end of the quay, immediately behind the last ship, I saw a queer-looking hut, surrounded by a few bushes. Near it several veiled women were bustling about.

"That is the tomb of Sheikh Barghut," Bill explained to me. "Some time at the beginning of the eighteenth century the swathed corpse of a man was washed ashore here and afterward burned on the beach by fishermen. The rumor went round that the body burned had been that of a saint, and it became the custom of boats to pour a little fresh water into the sea when they passed the place. *Barghut* means in the native language 'flea' or 'louse.' Apparently the man had been no bigger than a flea, and yet when they tried to pick him up, he had proved so heavy that he could not be moved from the spot. When the harbor was being laid out here, we wanted to put the tomb somewhere else. But the people ob-jected, so it stayed where it was. Today it is a popular place of pilgrimage for Sudanese ladies desirous of large families."

"And ahead there," he continued after we had gone a little further, pointing to the streaks of water alongside the pier that projected some way into the sea, "lie the submarine gar-dens, which you may have already heard of. We've a big ship here with a glass bottom, through which, for a few piasters, tourists can see the beds of coral. She's under repair at the moment. But of course the corals here in the harbor entrance can't even be remotely compared with those in the open sea yonder."

Meanwhile, a light haze began to rise. As soon as we had left the sheltered bottleneck of the harbor entrance behind, the swell had become noticeable. The police launch was not a good craft for such weather. She bumped straight into every wave crest, so that we were soon soaked through and through with spray. Bill had just cast his line overboard; suddenly he sprang backward with a curse.

"Damn it! Damn it! Damn it." he shouted. A rain of abuse descended upon the two seamen. A wave had struck Bill's pack of cigarettes which he had left lying in the open. Angrily, he hurled the sodden cigarettes, pack and all, overboard.

I wondered where we were going. The coastal reefs, at which I had been expecting to dive, were far behind our wake. We were now steering straight out to sea. Bill stood erect in the boat, with wind-blown hair, gripping his fishing rod. As he was obviously in a bad temper, I resolved to let events take the course he had in mind. The sea was amazingly warm. When a wave unexpectedly swept over my hand, I felt as though I were dipping it in warm bath water.

The Sudan coast now lay like a gray streak behind us, with the cranes of the harbor and the masts of the ships rising above the long red roofs of the warehouses. The range of hills in the distance stood out in more and more relief as the sun sank lower. Several hundred jagged peaks were visible over a wide area, the nearer ranges being darker, those further off, which touched the clouds, gleaming in the most delicate shades of blue.

We had been running on a straight course for a good half-hour without a single fish having taken any interest in Bill's line when surf, thrown up by a reef, rose before us. The end of the reef was marked by an iron signpost. Bill ordered the seamen to slacken speed.

"If you really want to dive here, you can do it now," he said, turning to me. "I should be very sorry, personally, if anything bumped into you, but it's up to you entirely."

"Can't we get a bit nearer the reef?" I asked. We were a good three hundred feet away from it.

"No, that's impossible; the sea's running too high."

This meant that I would have to dive overboard into the watery abyss and swim to the reef from the boat. The Commissioner, after his glance through my illustrations, seemed to be very confident of my capabilities. The present turn of affairs was by no means to my taste. It had been my intention to make myself acquainted with the new conditions by studying them carefully first from shallow water. Now I was in the middle of the Red Sea and seven years had gone by since I had last done any sea diving.

"I am really anxious and seriously worried about you," said Bill, watching me closely. "But I suppose you know what you're doing!"

All I could do to retain Bill's faith in my ability was to take a bite at this sour apple. I had already put on my swimming trunks; I quickly slipped on my fins, drew on my mask, gulped down my misgivings, and swung myself overboard. The boat went on, with Bill still fishing from it, and I remained behind. I glanced swiftly round under water. I could see nothing but dim, yawning, empty space in all directions. I was gliding over a sea chasm which might be three hundred or three thousand feet deep, for all I knew.

Thrashing away with my fins, I swam toward the reef, clearly recognizable from its streamers of foam. My heart was welling up into my throat. I had never before taken such a blind leap into the unknown. That I should enter upon my first submarine experience in the Red Sea holding part of a picture frame had certainly not been in my plan!

At last the first contours of sea bed became visible beneath me. The glimmering vision that rose up to meet me from the depths took my breath away. The bottom of the sea here, as it sloped upward before me out of blue nothingness to the steep wall of the reef, did not in the least resemble the coral floors I remembered in the Caribbean Sea. Platelike formations in the shape of projecting tables extended far and wide below me. Big, dark fish were ranged, all round them, motionless, exactly as though seated to take a meal at those enormous tables.

A little further on I found myself hovering, with relief, over a bottom I could clearly see. I felt safe again. Abysmal depths of water are not terrifying because they are easier to drown in than regions where the sea bed is visible at a depth of sixty feet, but because in vast depths of water there is no focal point to show, by comparison, how far one can see and at what distance a creature becomes visible when it is swimming toward one. As soon as one can get his bearings, either from a rock or even a small fish, the magic and sometimes eerie spell is immediately broken. He is then surrounded by a clearly delimited area, as though within the circle of a protective wall: there is a defined space that any enemy has to cross, thereby giving him a chance to arm and defend himself.

Floating along the surface like a bird soaring aloft, I looked down at the panorama below. Though the afternoon light was waning, I could see quite clearly. The multitude of variegated shapes and figures was so great that some time passed before I could distinguish details. In contrast with the West Indian reefs, which are mainly green, yellow, or brown, I could see here, despite the overcast brightness, that red was the predominant color. The elkhorn and staghorn varieties of coral were absent; instead of these, jagged points of Madrepora covered wide areas that resembled flower beds. They formed the tablelike structures and covered the tall, sturdy stems of other types of coral with tangled growths that bewildered the eye.

But I also found some old friends again: spherical Meandrina, looking like a human brain, and yellow "stinging corals" that grow up in platelike layers and will burn your fingers if you touch them. I particularly noted the complete absence of the soft sea whips, the plantlike growths found everywhere on the Caribbean reefs. In the Red Sea they are only represented by a few species which modestly shun the light and are only to be found at considerable depths or in the twilight of "chimneys" hollowed far into the reefs. On the other hand there were growths everywhere of Alcyonaria, which cover the hard-rock formations with the appearance of tattered leaves, graceful plumage, and moss in bloom.

I dived to thirty feet and discovered that my ears would now have to get used again to amphibious living. The water pressure was remarkably heavy. The Red Sea is not only the warmest but also the saltiest of the seas of the world.

I stopped at the foot of an overhanging, much perforated wall of reef and looked upward. Hundreds of infinitesimally small, glittering, red fish, each resembling a ruby, moved up and down the rock to the rhythm of the waves, silver streaks of slanting sunlight shooting among them like arrows. Blue, yellow, and brightly checkered parrot fishes played round the corals. Further back, in the deeper water, a shoal of rhinoceros fish, their heads adorned by a definite hornlike protuberance, were swimming. As I looked into a cavity close beside me I recognized the swinging pectoral fins of a spiny-rayed perch, speckled green and brown, and of remarkable size. Exactly as in any other sea, he lay there, sturdily built and clumsy, in front of his hole, his round eyes glaring at me.

I was particularly intrigued by some strangely oscillating formations, bright blue, that were peeping out between the corals. I swam nearer; the shapes contracted, as a fissure shrinks, and the double edge of bright blue disappeared. They were the open shells of large mussels, which were imbedded among the corals and had closed when I approached.

I kept perfectly still and then the mussels began to open again. It was obvious from their size that they were tridacnas, near relations of the giant clams one reads about in books on the South Seas, which are capable of seizing a diver's hand or foot between their hinged shells. On the Australian coast they may measure three feet in diameter and weigh two hundred pounds; they were smaller here. The keenness of their sensitivity to water vibration was amazing. A slight movement thirty feet away had been enough to make them close, just as if they had caught sight of me.

I dived about, completely oblivious of the world above. Many of the coral fishes looked as though the Almighty had been testing his whole palette on them, especially in the shallower water, where a whole menagerie was astir that would have delighted a collector of jewels. These swimming butterflies darted about so fast that I was often at a loss to know which was head and which tail at any given moment. They would burst unexpectedly out of one crevice and disappear into another before you could say "knife."

The entire mass of the reef was penetrated by a subterranean system of cavities that extended far out beneath the shallow water. In the mystic gloom of the grottoes grotesque masks were outlined against the walls. Many lay in close contact with the coral rock itself; these were sponges and Bryozoa, arranged in fantastic patterns. Others were making off, under sail, in sudden flight: they were the irregularly shaped frogfish or hideous, broad-headed Scorpaenidae, which lie in wait for their prey close against the rock.

Time was passing. I had already been a good three-quarters of an hour in the water. I had completely forgotten Bill. I looked round for him and saw that the boat was searching for me. I hid myself near the reef and then took a long dive, so that I didn't come up again until I was right under the boat's side.

"Oh, so there you are at last!" cried Bill, in a tone of relief. "We've been looking for you everywhere! Where on earth did you go to? I'm horribly cold and I've been wanting to get back for ages!"

I apologized and asked what luck he had had.

"Oh, absolutely none at all. One can't do anything with this old tub. The engine's always stalling and the sea's running too high. I soon gave up, and for the last half-hour we've done nothing but look for you!"

To cheer him up I described the wonders I had seen in the depths of the sea.

"Well, and what about sharks?" he interrupted.

"No, not one of them turned up. Next time I'll take a spare mask with me and then you must have a look at the reef too."

"I'll be damned if I do such a thing," he growled back. "If you're so set on finishing up in a shark's belly, that's your affair. None of them's going to eat me!"

We followed the setting sun back to the harbor. The waves were now behind us and sent us along at a good round speed. We each had a bath when we got home, to wash the salt off. Then we drove to the English Club, where the eighty English people living in Port Sudan played billiards or cards; drank whisky or beer; bathed in a big modern swimming pool; or in the evening, danced the English waltz, the tango, or the samba on the concrete floor of an annex illuminated by Chinese lanterns.

At the bar, over a glass of whisky, I was introduced to the harbor master, his wife, and a number of other people. Bill was obviously the center of social life here. He was greeted everywhere with "hello's," and I was astonished at the rapidity with which he neatly turned our afternoon excursion into an anecdote representing me as a kind of bewitched seal, who jumped overboard in mid-ocean, armed with only a picture frame, and bobbed up again a whole hour later out of abysmal depths.

"You must positively pay a visit to Flamingo Bay—the Port Sudan harbor for sailing craft—one of these days," the harbor master told me. "They've got a crab on the beach there which attaches itself by its pincers to the fins of small fish and makes them take it for a ride through the sea. I've seen it done myself, but none of these people believe me."

He looked round the circle of faces with an exceedingly mournful expression. Everyone laughed and raised their glasses to him.

"Go a little further north," said another man. "There are sea cows there that hold their young right up above water and suckle them. You photograph that and you'll make a sensation!"

An elderly woman rose from her seat and came over to us. "You ought to have been here last year! A whale got into the harbor and you might have been able to get it out again."

"On a string!" laughed the harbor master. Everyone bent double with glee.

"No, but I really mean that," the lady declared defiantly. "That blood bath we had could certainly have been avoided!"

"A whale?" I asked.

"Yes. The poor beast had wandered into the harbor somehow and couldn't get out again; and in the end the Fuzzies attacked it in shallow water with their swords, cut it to pieces, and the whole town had it to eat." She glanced reproachfully at Bill, who was just ordering more whiskies.

"I forbade them to do it," Bill said.

"But then you let them do it just the same!"

"Yes, but only because the beast was pretty well dead by that time and the whole harbor was beginning to stink!"

I heard that it was a whale twenty-five feet long, the only specimen that had been seen in the neighborhood for many years.

I was dead tired and quite pleased when we took our leave. I had had little sleep in the aircraft, and on top of that had come the change of climate and the first descent under water. Bill told me, when we reached home, that the Governor was on a visit to Port Sudan and had asked us to dine with him at the Red Sea Hotel.

"Did he ask me too?" I inquired.

"Yes, of course. He even made a special point of requesting me to bring you along. He is a nice old boy, who incidentally knows a deuce of a lot about fishing."

In my room Achmed had laid out my evening clothes on the bed; beside the bed, on the floor, lay my patent-leather shoes; to the right a silk shirt and black tie; to the left, my socks, turned inside out in such a way that I could easily slip them on. The whole arrangement indicated exemplary neatness of mind and a decided passion for symmetry. I shaved, sighing, and wormed my way into this funereal toggery. Lucky I'd thought of bringing the things!

We drank yet another whisky in the drawing room, then we drove to the Red Sea Hotel, where the other guests were already waiting for us on the first-floor terrace. The ladies wore long evening frocks, while the gentlemen, with the exception of Bill, who was in white dinner clothes, had on black trousers, short-sleeved shirts, black ties, and broad silk scarves round their waists.

"Don't hesitate to take your coat off," the Governor said encouragingly, after giving me a friendly greeting. He was a gentleman of indeterminate age, fond of clearing his throat before speaking.

I asked what the scarves were for and what they meant.

"We call them cummerbunds," he told me. "It keeps your

stomach warm, which is important in the tropics. Otherwise you easily get a chill."

The food was rather better than at Bill's. Dinner was to be followed by a visit of the whole party to the movie theater. But just as we were about to leave, it began to rain; it came down so hard that the ladies, in their long dresses, were reluctant to leave the doorway. Great regret was expressed, for a film was being shown with Clark Gable, whom all the ladies adored. When the downpour slackened a little, we scurried into the cars. But on our arrival at the theater the rain was again coming down so hard that to alight was out of the question. We waited five minutes, then we drove back to the hotel and one of the ladies began to tell our fortunes from a pack of cards.

My recollections of this last part of the evening are a bit vague, for I was in such a condition that I had to exercise all my will power to keep from falling asleep where I sat. Gradually, with excruciating delays, each of us learned what his future was to be and the kind of dark lady he was going to meet shortly. At last the Governor rose and announced that it was time to go to bed.

At home I was just able to fling my evening clothes across a chair. Then I slept like the dead. I dreamed of the Governor swimming across a reef, accompanied by a multitude of brightly colored fishes, and clearing his throat repeatedly. I was anxious to tell him something, but he couldn't hear me. Then everything vanished in the total darkness of a turbid sea.

THE WRECK

THE WRECK

A SHRILL CLATTER, somewhere near my head, woke me. Achmed, uttering amiably guttural noises, was placing a small teapot, a cup, and a little plate containing three sweet biscuits on the table by my bed. It was just half-past six. I could have murdered the fellow. I was still deeply exhausted, and now I certainly couldn't get to sleep again. This waking of people with nothing more than tea and three sweet biscuits is a typically English custom. One then assents to getting up, goes for a little stroll in the garden, and at eight or half-past devours a huge breakfast.

Sunbeams sparkled among the brightly colored curtains. The scent of creepers in bloom drifted through the open door of the balcony. Achmed had switched on the big propeller in the middle of the ceiling in my room, and it turned slowly, sending down cool wafts of air in my direction. As summer advances and the heat increases, the propeller is adjusted to greater speed till at last it hums, night and day, like a giant bumblebee.

I went out on the balcony. Down in the garden Bill, in his dressing gown, was inspecting his flowers. The chauffeur, whose name was also Achmed, was polishing the car; he looked up at me and saluted.

"We're having breakfast at eight," Bill called up to me when he saw me. "The Governor and his wife are coming. How did you sleep?"

"Very well indeed. But unfortunately not quite long enough."

A half-hour later Bill had put on full ceremonial dress. He wore a white, gold-laced uniform and shoes that seemed a bit tight for him. He told me that he only donned this finery on very special occasions. The Governor was coming again, that afternoon, to tea, and would be leaving Port Sudan in the evening.

Breakfast was a formal meal. I was much interested in what the Governor told me about an island further to the north, which he had visited himself two years before. It seemed that on one side of the island there was a perpendicular cliff more than three hundred feet high. From its edge the Governor had seen over a hundred sharks at once, drumming about in the shallow, sandy water.

"Over a hundred?" I inquired, as respectfully as I could.

The Governor cleared his throat.

"There must have been more than a hundred. The water was full of them. I saw a rather similar sight once before, I remember. It must be quite fifteen years ago now. It was at the island of Talla Talla, which lies to the south, further down toward Eritrea. The water there was so full of sharks that you could stick an oar into the water and it would stay upright. What they were up to I don't know. It might have been their mating season. But anyhow the sea was chock-full of them."

"And were the sharks at the other island, the one to the north, big ones?"

"Yes, some of them were quite handsome fellows. Six and even nine feet long, I'm sure. I'm convinced that if you visited the place you'd certainly find a lot to look at."

"It's the finest fishing ground on the whole coast," Bill added.

The island was situated, I was told, about a hundred miles to the north, near Muhammad Qol. I made a mental note not to forget to go there. The island of Talla Talla, to the south, could only be reached in a fairly large vessel, but you could drive by car through the desert to Muhammad Qol and thence cross to the isle of sharks by boat.

The Governor and his wife rose from the table, thanked their host, and departed. Bill picked up a little case which contained his most important papers and went out to his car, by which Achmed the chauffeur was standing at attention. If I would like to call at his office to get my visa extended, he observed, he would send the car to fetch me later on.

"Couldn't I come with you right away?" I asked. "I've got my passport on me."

"Certainly," Bill answered and made room for me in the car.

I sat down beside him and was sorry the very next moment that I had been in such a hurry. I suddenly remembered that Bill was the highest-ranking British Government representative in the town and probably his drive to his office was an official affair, that being the reason he had wanted to send the car for me later.

As we swept up to the government building in a wide arc, bugle calls rang out. Achmed opened the door of the car, Bill and I got out, and before a numerous crowd of attentive Arabs, eight Sudanese soldiers presented arms. The bugler blared away for all he was worth; the soldiers executed two brisk turns, stepped back, and the relieving guard marched up. Bill stood like a statue, saluting the flag.

I stood a few steps behind Bill, the cynosure of all eyes, and though filled with the best intentions, I still had no idea what to do with myself. I could stand at attention all right, but I could hardly salute in civilian clothes, with no hat on. Bill signed to me to follow him. We passed some more Sudanese soldiers who presented arms, went up the wide staircase to the first floor, and entered the Commissioner's reception room.

Bill then discarded his official expression and sent for the passport officer, whom he instructed to see to my extension. The application would have to be sent to Khartoum, but he would himself recommend approval of it. He showed me a glass case containing every species of Red Sea mussel, in particular pearl mussels of all sizes, arranged in rows. But I sensed he had a great deal to do and so took my leave without delay.

The chief of police, to whom Bill had sent me, gave orders that I was to be supplied with a suitable boat. As to the cost, he said he would negotiate with the owner himself on my behalf, to prevent my being cheated. The boat, a felucca, would be ready for me at one o'clock.

I had still a lot to do before then. At the Red Sea Hotel, situated only a few hundred yards from the Government House, I ordered a cold lunch to take with me in the boat.

Then I paid a hurried visit to Barclay's Bank, where I found that my remittance from Vienna had duly arrived. I asked to be directed to the largest drugstore in town, where I thought I might be able to get hold of some soda and lime which can be used as well as caustic soda for the respirator.

On my way to the druggist's I was greeted everywhere by clamoring merchants who wanted to sell me something and by ragged children who ran along beside me, holding out their hands and begging. In order to get rid of them, I distributed a few coins. But that was the signal for a much worse pandemonium; far and wide, like bees to a tree in bloom, children and beggars came swarming round and only left me when a Negro policeman came to my rescue.

In an Arab café, from which came the shrill, dissonant sounds of oriental music played by a phonograph, I saw a cripple who had lost both arms. He sat on the floor, leaning against the wall, and was gossiping with another ragged individual. When he noticed me and saw I was looking at him, he stretched out one of his legs and picked up with his toes a bottle of lemonade which was standing on a chair and raised it dexterously to his mouth. I stood still, whereupon the other instantly hauled a few absolutely filthy playing cards out of his pocket and both began to play with them; the armless man was actually able to shuffle the cards with his toes. He also used his toes to pocket the coin I threw him.

At the drugstore, a great musty place with all sorts of dusty bottles in it, I could find nothing suitable as a substitute for the caustic soda. The white-haired druggist searched his books and said he could get what I wanted, but the price he quoted was so high and the probable date of delivery so uncertain that I declined his offer and gave up my idea.

At one o'clock I arrived with my equipment and lunch at the little pier in the harbor. As all I could see were a number of rowboats used as ferries to cross the harbor, I asked the Negro sentry on guard in his box whether he had seen the felucca I was waiting for. But the man did not understand English. And all I knew of his language was the word "felucca." All the owners of boats came swarming up and volunteered to row me across the harbor at cut-rate prices, but I couldn't get the information I wanted out of them.

Some Fuzzies were lounging about on the pier in picturesque attitudes. In and out of the brightly colored weeds, against the pier's stone wall, darted the same bright-hued little fishes that I already knew. Finally a boat, larger than the rest, sailed up. It was built on rakish lines, some fifteen feet long and rather narrow. The mast slanted forward in the Arab style. The pointed sail was relatively small. As the vessel came alongside, I saw that some pretty little mats had been laid out on the deck.

The crew consisted of two tattooed natives, one with an extremely ferocious, and the other with an extremely crafty, expression. The latter was evidently the spokesman. He jumped nimbly ashore, saluted me by laying his hands against his chest and forehead, and gave me to understand that his name was Mahmud and that he was very much at my service.

The second man moored the boat and then greeted me in a similar manner. He grinned and the ferocious expression melted away. In its place a semblance of simple childlike awe, somewhat uncomprehending, settled. Clearly he was anxious to please and impress me but a bit at a loss for the correct way to proceed. Throughout our acquaintance he wore only these two expressions. I later decided the ferocity was really only the visible evidence of his determination to succeed at, and his concentration on, the task at hand. Mahmud informed me that his colleague's name was O Sheik.

My gear was stowed in the boat and I lay down on the mats. Mahmud steered and gave the orders; O Sheik crouched forward and hauled the sheet. We soon left the shore and the grinning crowd of spectators behind. We crossed the harbor with the sail bellying and took the same course as the motorboat had taken the day before.

As we approached the outer pier, where the submarine gardens were situated, Mahmud gave me to understand that this would be a good place to dive. I replied to him by signs that I did not want to dive here but away to the left in front of the harbor, close to the lateral coastal reef. Both men appeared utterly dumfounded by this news. Mahmud snapped at the air, with eyes rolling, and shook his head vigorously, to illustrate the fate that awaited all who dared to enter the water in that direction. His face was a study. I could clearly see in it a mixture of pleasure at having found a foreigner who paid well and deep apprehension at the prospect of losing him again so very soon.

"*Girsch! Girsch ḳabir!*" he kept repeating. From the look of him it seemed as though the sharks over there must really be pretty savage.

"*Kois, ḳalas,*" I answered. Those were the only words I had learned so far. They meant, "Good, that's all right."

The leftward fringe of reefs started right in front of the pier and ran parallel to the coast in a long, only slightly wavering line. As could be seen from the conspicuous difference in the color of the water, the reef fell perpendicularly into the depths of the sea from a level twenty-five or thirty feet below the surface. We sailed right over this level, where the water suddenly turned to an intense blue. Between this spot and a wall of rock in shallow water against which the waves broke, lay an area from 100 to 150 feet wide, over which corals, growing high from a gently shelving bottom, gleamed with all the colors of the rainbow. Beyond the rocks lay a lagoon, several hundred yards wide, which those who wished to reach the reef from the coastal desert had to ford. The water in the lagoon could only be about three feet deep. It glistened in green and yellow hues.

I gave the signal to cast anchor in a tiny cove that broke the straight line of the reef. Neither of the members of my crew was much impressed by this proceeding. They were obviously afraid that the anchor would not hold and the wind would drive the craft onto the rocks in the shallows. But I calmed them down, explaining in pantomime that I would myself make the anchor fast on the bottom.

I was overboard in an instant.

Now in the clear midday sunlight the effect of the splendid coloring of the corals was still more striking than it had been in the late afternoon. Right beneath me I could see the glimmer of a bushy growth tinted like a peach; from Klunzinger's descriptions I recognized it at once as a cupstar coral. Pen corals were spreading around me in bluish-violet bouquets. Among them I found a cinnabar-red Coenopsammia. Dozens of different species of star corals grew in bright globes and bunches. Snow-white thistle corals filled the cavities. Crown corals bristled with pointed branches of delicate rose color. And the bright-hued coral fishes, too, darted like butterflies about this Elysian garden.

The place where we had cast anchor was less than thirty feet away from the fall of the sea bed. I swam over the ledge. Here the wall of the reef really dropped perpendicularly into the depths, so far down that in spite of the clarity of the water I couldn't see the base. I could well believe that, as Mahmud had said, sharks frequented the place. I decided to put off a closer examination of this precipice until some other time when I should be using my respirator, and to limit myself on this occasion to the corals in the shallows.

I fixed our anchor between two great blocks of coral, where it would be impossible for it to break loose, and climbed back into the boat again. In order to test the cover of my submarine camera before using it, I took the cover off, screwed it up empty, and lowered it into the water at the end of a rope. A little later, when I opened it, I was able to ascertain that it was watertight. Then I took pencil and paper and made a note of all the photographs I wished to take, for I intended to devote this first day to the study of conditions of light and the effects of different types of special filter.

Mahmud and O Sheik watched everything I did with great attention. The waterproof cover, in particular, seemed to intrigue them. When I let it down into the water with the rope, O Sheik's lips parted in a broad grin. In spite of his respect for me he couldn't help bursting into a laugh at the behavior of this foreigner who was so naïve as to try and catch fish with that sort of bait.

As soon as I had the camera properly encased in its waterproof cover again, I slid overboard once more. As I had to open the cover each time I took a photograph, in order to change the filter, an hour passed before my task was finished. Conditions of light were by no means easy here. Though the water at the lower depths was beautifully clear, just below the surface myriads of microscopic organisms were floating, turning the water to a kind of thick broth and only letting the sunlight through to an extent which depended on the density of the particular mass.

I noted, without any particular pleasure, that here too one encountered those tiny jellyfish, invisible to the naked eye, which can sting you quite appreciably without your being able to do anything about it. While I was taking my photographs, I kept glancing behind and all around me. I should have been glad to see my first shark; for so long as I didn't see one, I shouldn't know whether sharks in this neighborhood really behaved any differently than elsewhere.

After eating some of my lunch in the boat, I put a new film in my Leica and went off on another camera hunt. Fortune favored me at once. A big tropical jellyfish, the medusa, opalescently tinted in exquisite blues, drifted toward me. It came swimming through the water with pulsating, rhythmical movements of its bell-like shape, dragging an enormous quantity of long stinging-threads behind it. The marginal tufts spread out sideways like yellow pedicels.

As I swam nearer, I saw some tiny fish playing hide and seek under the screen of the medusa's great bell, in among the dangerous tentacles. They are called shepherd fish, and it is one of nature's miracles that the greedy medusa spares and even protects them. While I was taking my photograph, two or three of them emerged from the forest of long threads, inquisitively examined the glittering lens, and dashed back again, when I moved, into their safe refuge.

The strong current was driving the medusa toward the

reefs in the shallows, and I followed it till it stranded and was torn to pieces on the sharp points of the dead stumps of coral. The little fishlets then didn't know where to go. They dashed around the rock and hid themselves in the fragments that remained. It was tragedy in miniature, repeated a thousandfold every second in the sea.

Even in quite shallow water, where the plateau of the reef had been worn smooth by the powerful surf, larger fish were darting to and fro. They were mostly blue and brown surf fish, many with an exceedingly beautiful design in yellow on the head. Excited snipefish emerged from shallow cavities, shooting about all over the place. Immediately below the surface a shoal of young arrow pike was dashing along, looking like long, thin knitting needles. Fat blue parrot fish tried to nibble a piece of coral every time the water ceased its surge for a moment. But all this went on in such an excited and hurried manner that decent photographs were out of the question.

Here, too, clams were much in evidence. Many were posted, like open calyxes, on the tops of tall, towerlike lace-work corals. I got hold of one and tried to pull it off. But I was too slow in grabbing at it. The creature had become aware of the danger and had had time to stiffen the muscle with which it clung to the rock. When I looked at my hand, I saw that I had cut several of my fingers on the sharp edges. I had my harpoon handed to me from the boat and lay in wait. When I saw the shells opening again, I lunged like lightning with the blunt end and the mussel dropped. I cut it open with my knife. Dozens of little fishes dashed up and scuffled over the soft parts. Today, as I write, the shells are on my desk, serving as ashtrays.

Suddenly, I heard both Mahmud and O Sheik call out. They had been making themselves comfortable in the boat; now I saw the two of them, in their white nightshirt garments, jump overboard like poodles. One of them got hold of the boat; the other, kicking out hard, disappeared under water and came up again presently, puffing and struggling. The anchor had dragged, the rope having been rubbed through against the two blocks of coral. I hurried to their assistance. The boat had already been driven, in those few seconds, quite a way toward the rocks in the shallows. As it was blowing fairly hard over the reef, we had to use all our strength to keep the vessel from stranding.

When the three of us were once again aboard, we laughed to think we had all gotten so excited. Good-humoredly, I committed the enormity of offering Mahmud a ham roll, which he, as a good Moslem, declined with as much amiability as firmness. As a substitute he produced a small box of chewing tobacco and stuck a sizeable chunk of it in his mouth. He fingered my harpoon and asked me by signs what it was for. I was only too delighted to give him a practical illustration!

I ought to have been content, for the first day, with my photographic booty; but now a fish, too, had to meet its doom. Achmed had supplied me with a new shaft that morning, so I was no longer dependent on the picture-frame molding. Accordingly, I left the camera in the boat and dived cautiously overboard.

But it was by no means easy to outwit a fish down here. Though one can shoot down a fish at a five- or ten-foot range with a submarine catapult—such catapults are in use today on many coasts of the world—one has to get within a foot or two of him with a spear, to be able to run him through with a sudden lunge. It is true that this kind of hunting is less productive, but for that very reason it is all the more interesting.

To be able to outwit individual species, one has to become a real expert on the nature of the beast. In addition one has no mechanical advantage over the fish. The first thing I had to do was to refresh my memory concerning the pattern of the inaudible movements which one has to employ to sneak through the water. The slightest splashing frightens the fish, especially in regions swarming with other fish, for if one of them notices anything, his panic affects all the rest.

I missed my mark several times; then I saw a big red fish lying motionless under a rock and determined that he and no other was destined to grace Bill Clark's dinner menu.

I drew a long breath and plunged to a plateau, some distance away, where a perpendicular perforation, like a gun barrel, sank through the reef. I slipped into this opening and dodged, like a deerstalker, behind the big block of coral, on the opposite side of which lay the fish in his den.

Halfway round the coral block two little parrot fish came to meet me, one of them swimming directly into the line of my harpoon. I had to hang on tight to the coral and remain motionless, otherwise I should have frightened the fish—and then my chances would have been ruined. But the pair seemed to know what my game was and amused themselves by performing a series of flashing somersaults under my nose. After a while they got tired of entertaining and swam on their way. I slipped swiftly round the rock. Heaven be praised! The fish still lay in the same place. A little distance behind him a small crab was burrowing with his claws in a hole full of sand.

I pushed cautiously in between two corals. Then I sent the harpoon whizzing forward with all my strength. As I did so, I not only hit the fish right through his middle, but also banged my elbow against a coral with such force that for a moment I could neither hear nor see anything.

I had no time to worry about this bruise, however, for just above my head a long, thin body had appeared. Its pointed snout seemed to be looking right down at me. A shark! It was, to be sure, the smallest I had ever seen. He was less than a yard in length and was more like a fat mischievous pike than the dreaded killer whose name he bore. He turned away and vanished. As the fish had gotten tangled up with my line among the corals, I rose rapidly to the surface for a breath of air. Then I saw the shark again. He was now gliding away over the sloping mass of coral and up again toward the place where my fish lay.

No doubt he wanted to take the prize for himself!

I was down again in a moment and disentangled the line. Mahmud was beside himself with delight when he saw me come over the side with my gorgeously colored prize.

An hour later I was sitting at tea with Bill and the Governor and the fish was shown round. He was a Holocentrus, or squirrel fish, weighing about eight pounds. Mahmud had assured me that he would be a first-rate dish for the table.

"And so the shark wanted to get the fish away from you?" inquired the Governor's wife excitedly.

I told her that you could hardly call that particular shark a real one.

"Oh, but you must really go and dive down to the *Um-*

brea," she cried. "I'm certain you would have the most incredible experiences!"

Bill explained that the *Umbrea* was a big Italian ship which had gone down about a mile from Port Sudan. The tops of both her masts were still visible above water. It was, however, strictly forbidden to go near the wreck.

"Is there much gold aboard then?" I asked.

"No, not gold, but dynamite. No less than seven thousand tons of munitions and explosives."

The Governor cleared his throat. "The *Umbrea* was taking her cargo to Eritrea," he said. "She was lying at anchor here on the very day that Italy entered the war against us. We took over the vessel and the Italians were just about to leave, when suddenly it was announced, with great excitement, that the *Umbrea* was sinking. The Italians had managed, despite our vigilance, to break open the bulkheads. The ship could nevertheless have been easily salvaged, but we were informed that they had also set time fuses, so there was nothing to do but let her sink."

"She's lying at a depth of from 60 to 120 feet," said Bill. "You can see her hull under water quite clearly from the surface. In any case there are still about half a million Maria Theresa thalers aboard. It was not until last year that an Italian salvage firm applied for permission to raise the vessel. But we refused to grant it."

"Why was that?"

"Because the view of the Admiralty is that the ship might still suddenly blow up any day."

"Blow up? Under water?"

"Yes. Some fuses get rusted through in the course of time, and then the danger of spontaneous combustion arises. According to the best authorities on the subject, the critical time is during the first ten to fifteen years—and that is right now! We considered the idea of blowing up the vessel ourselves, as it's blocking the entire anchorage of the outer Wingate, but that proved impracticable. At Government House we've got a professional opinion seventeen pages long, drawn up by two officers who came here to study the subject. If the *Umbrea* blew up, the whole of the eastern area of Port Sudan would be flooded. Seven thousand tons of dynamite, after all, are no laughing matter."

I couldn't get this wreck out of my head. At dinner I raised the question again and asked Bill whether he could possibly get a diving permit for me. He said he would be willing enough to try but advised me at the same time not to entertain any great hopes of it. The harbor master, he explained, had his own ideas on the subject. He would certainly be afraid that I would send the whole ship up and Port Sudan with it.

"But I won't touch anything," I said. "All I want to do is to take a few photographs, which would be of great scientific interest. For, since we know how long the ship has been lying on the bottom, we can calculate how long the individual corals which have grown up on the wreck have taken to develop. And it would also be interesting to know what fishes have located themselves there. Interesting conclusions could be drawn from such information."

Bill promised to do his best.

After dinner we went together to the open-air movie to see an American film. All European producers ought to witness such a presentation just once, to add to their store of knowledge. The ten front rows, packed with Sudanese, Fuz-

Mahmud, his face tattooed in keeping with the native custom, proved himself an able seaman and fisherman, as well as a great rascal.

Mahmud, O Sheik, and I explored the sea around Port Sudan in this rakish, fifteen-foot felucca whose mast slants forward, in the Arab style.

I glided down to the sunken *Umbrea* where corals had already grown into flowerlike shapes and fastened everywhere over the old ironwork. And what had this been — the ship's bell? Or searchlight?

The railings running about the partly rotted deck were festooned with bushy coral clusters which had achieved amazing proportions in the nine years the ship had lain under the Red Sea.

A butterfly fish, striped black and yellow, hovered about the windlass of the sunken ship. Could it be that it liked windlasses because the numerous chinks in the machine afforded a safe refuge?

The broken, rotted ladder led to the interior of the vessel, and I made my way through the murky, dimly lighted passageways.

At the bottom of the hold I found the dreaded cargo — seven thousand tons of munitions!

zies, and Arabs, shouted and yelled every time a horse gal-
loped across the screen and every time a white woman, with
a languishing air, sank into her lover's arms. The plot was a
matter of utter indifference to the public.

When, later on, we saw a film at the same theater where
the sequences had been transposed—the same man first died
and then fell ill—the manager, when we drew his attention
to this, replied that he had now been showing the film in this
way for three days and this was the first time anyone had
mentioned the point to him. Everyone had been perfectly
satisfied hitherto.

Next morning I sailed with my two faithful comrades to
the same reef where I dived that first afternoon. From this
spot I could clearly distinguish, some distance away, the two
mastheads of the *Umbrea,* showing just above water. They
were slanting a little, at an angle of about 45°; the vessel,
then, must be lying on the bottom with a considerable list. I
wondered whether I should ever be able to get permission
to visit it. Then I pulled myself out of my reverie and gave
the order to cruise along the reef for a bit. It stood in the sea
like a long, curving wall. We anchored at a promising spot.

The sea bed fell away at that point very close to the reef,
so that our craft swung at anchor about five feet from the
cliffs. The water was calm and what wind there was came
from the other side. This time I had brought my diving gear.
But I did not use it. I swam along beside the cliffs, examined
corals, and took several photographs of fish; I kept thinking
all the time about the sunken ship. It was lying almost
within arm's length, and yet I couldn't visit it on account of
that stupid prohibition.

In my distraction I turned the film for the final photographs with such force that the end came away from the spool. If I wanted to put in a new film for further use, I must open the camera in my light-proof, change-over bag and try to roll the spool back by hand. I got back into the boat and groped with both hands in the black-cloth pouch, which had double elastic on both sides, so that not the least glimmer of light could penetrate it. It proved extremely difficult to roll the film back. The end had caught somewhere and was stuck fast in the camera. The longer I struggled, the more the sun burned my back, and my hands began to perspire in the tightly closed bag.

I cursed under my breath. I had now gotten the film partially free and couldn't take my hands out of the bag before I had finished the job. I began to tug viciously, the sweat running off my fingers, and I could feel one picture after the other being spoiled by their touch. At last I got into such a rage that I tore the whole wretched film out of the bag and heaved it into the sea. All my painful efforts had gone for nothing! And I'd gotten sunburn on my back in the bargain!

"Up with the sail!" I ordered. "We're going off over yonder." I pointed to the masts of the sunken ship.

It was really too absurd for words. Port Sudan was only visible from this spot as a reddish streak. How could anyone there see exactly where our nutshell of a craft was anchored?

Mahmud seemed worried at my command. He waved and wagged his hands, and rolled his eyes dramatically; I knew he was trying to tell me that boats were not allowed near the wreck and the risk of an explosion was very great. I repeated the order in an even sharper tone, and Mahmud relayed it to O Sheik, who had been watching and listening warily. He too seemed a little dubious about the turn of events. Both with fearful protestations hurried to do my bidding.

The wind was in our favor and we went off with our sail bellying. We negotiated a gap in the long wall of the reef and reached the sunken vessel within ten minutes. The ends of the masts, as they rose diagonally from the water, came up much higher than I suspected, now that I saw them close at hand. The upper side of the iron had been varnished white with the droppings of the many sea birds that continually perched on it. As we steered in and made our boat fast to a dangling steel hawser, they fluttered up and circled above our heads, screaming loudly.

I leaned over the side. In spite of the waves I could clearly distinguish the outlines of the massive hull. I felt like a knight of olden days who had stumbled upon an enchanted castle and was just about to enter it.

My hands shook as I strapped on my diving equipment and screwed up my submarine camera. Then I changed my mind. I would go down first with my spear only and leave the camera aboard for the time being. Mahmud and O Sheik watched me, wide-eyed. They both tried to give me some information connected with the wreck. So far as I could gather from their gestures, there were some female sea spirits living down there, which were no doubt very fascinating, but also very dangerous. The devil there were, I thought. But all the better . . . . .

Mahmud helped me buckle the straps tight. Then I sucked the respirator empty, pumped in oxygen from the cylinder at my belt, put on my nose clamp, spat into the mask (to keep the glass from misting), rinsed it out, and pulled it over my eyes. I already had my fins on. O Sheik handed me the spear. According to the manometer at my belt I had enough oxygen to stay under water for a good hour. At the last moment I noticed that the stopper of the oxygen cylinder was not quite tight, but the loss of gas was very slight, and I had no mind to unstrap my gear to make an adjustment; so overboard I went.

This was my first descent in diving gear for seven years. That it should take me aboard a sunken ship was hardly what I had dreamed of in Vienna. The pleasure of swimming under water again and at the same time being able to breathe freely was a wonderful feeling. With this type of gear I could sink into the depths of the sea, not like a clumsy diver, but as though transformed into an actual fish, gliding about with ease in this three-dimensional world.

In the process it is not necessary to pay much attention to mechanical details. If there isn't enough air in the bag, all that is necessary is to press the valve at one's belt and fresh oxygen flows in. When going deeper, this must be done again because the deeper one goes the more the weight of the water compresses the gas. Bouyancy decreases and so with ever increasing body weight, you drop downward like a plummet. If you swim up again, the oxygen in the bag expands as the pressure of the water decreases, and it is then necessary, in order to get rid of the excess gas and to keep the tightly inflated bag from bursting, to blow air out through a corner of your mouth. And so in the midst of an ever widening stream of air bubbles you shoot to the surface like a balloon.

I glided over a blue-black abyss. Below, to my right, lay the steeply sloping, precipitous deck of the steamer, one side rising comparatively high, the other lost in the invisible chasm. The massive, cylindrical funnel slanted upward to one side, surrounded by all sorts of superstructures and a wildly tangled mass of steam pipes and air tubes. Corals had fastened everywhere over the old ironwork and even over the stretched wire ropes; already they had grown into flower-like shapes. Among them swam innumerable brightly colored fishes, which seemed to feel just as much at home here as around a coral reef.

I hastened to get clear of the open water. I sailed in a slanting glide onto the middle of the deck.

At a depth of sixty feet I settled easily, like a bird, on a steam pipe and stayed there for some minutes, taking in the impression of my environment as a whole. The ship appeared in fact to be a very large one, as it rested here on the lap of the Red Sea under a growth of coral that resembled a sweet-brier hedge. I could well imagine what it would look like here in fifty or a hundred years. The corals, like creepers, would then have covered the entire hull and closed most of the open doors and hatches. And in two hundred years the ship would no longer be anything more than an oddly shaped coral reef in which, to be sure, enough dynamite lay buried to blow up a whole city and enough silver to build a good deal of it up again.

A shoal of coral fish, striped yellow and black, swam up to me at a great rate and surrounded me. My mask and the thin stream of bubbles that rose like beads from the loosely fastened part of the cylinder stopper appeared to arouse their interest. A particularly fat one swam inquisitively after the bubbles and dodged between them like a boy playing about under a shower bath.

85

The whole shoal followed its brother adventurer in a wedge formation, then it veered suddenly away, and hurried back to its former environs—a great capstan, well encrusted with coral.

As the planks of the deck had partly rotted away, I could see right through the iron girders to the deck below. The railings were festooned with bushy coral clusters which had grown to amazing size during the nine years the vessel had lain under water. However, other corals, spherical in shape, had only attained the dimensions of a child's fist.

From my steam pipe I could see the two masts, which, in their towering slant to the sea heavens, ceased to be visible the moment they rose above water. Between me and the silhouette of our felucca which floated high overhead, a big barracuda hung motionless near one of the mast ends. Most of the other fishes I saw were blue surgeonfish, butterfly fish, various kinds of parrot fishes, and black and yellow angelfish. Close beside me, round the spherical mass of adjacent steam pipes, tiny red fish occasionally formed a garland. After taking due note of all this, I left my steam pipe and went gliding down through the gaps in the iron girders to the lower deck.

The light was a bit dimmer down there. I put my head on one side, so as to look straight along the passageway, and tried to imagine the sailors who had once passed to and fro there. To my right a door gave access to a dark interior. I waited until my eyes had grown accustomed to the gloom, then I crossed the threshold.

The space within was faintly illuminated from the door and two window openings. As the floor slanted, like every other part of the decks, loose lumber had gotten heaped up on the opposite side and was covered with slime, reminding me of a collection of hideous cuttlefish. A table in the center of the room was screwed down tight, so it hadn't been disturbed. I slid over to it, then saw something round and glittering overhead. It was an electric-light bulb! I tried to unscrew it, but it was slimy and stuck fast with rust.

Suddenly, the door was darkened.

A fat, spiny-rayed perch was hovering on the threshold, staring in. For some reason the sight of it made me realize the solemn silence that weighed down the dead hull of the ship. Perhaps it was because I had seen another spiny-rayed perch the day before, on the wave-washed coral reef. Here it was as quiet as the grave. Though hitherto the multiplicity of impressions had left me no time at all to experience fear, I now felt the chill of goose skin all over my body. The water was noticeably cooler here than out in the open depths away from the ship. The perch drifted irresolutely across the threshold, then he gave a start and darted out again with a sudden flick of his tail. The abrupt, clearly audible sound he made lingered for some time in the oppressive stillness.

I shook off the shrinking feeling in my chest. By a side door—at its corner rather than its upper part, owing to the slant of the deck—I swam to an adjoining room, and thence, by still another door, to a tiny, almost wholly dark bathroom. The bathtub had been beautifully enameled in white and was still fairly bright; its appearance struck me as being so grotesquely comic that I laughed aloud into my respirator and went and sat down in the thing.

From the slanting ceiling overhead two thin plates projected, hanging downward. I touched them cautiously. Unlike the tarnished mirror on the wall to my right, these platelike shapes were not part of the former furniture of the place. They were mussels. In fact, they were real pearl mussels, as I could see on closer examination. I had a knife with me, and I cut one of them open. I scraped away the bleeding flesh with my fingers, wondering whether there might be a pearl inside. That would have been an experience that I should never be able to get anyone to believe; that I had sat in a bathtub on a sunken ship in mid-sea and pried a pearl loose from a mussel on the ceiling!

Unfortunately, there was no pearl to be found. Instead, some little fish appeared and began scuffling in the dark over the flesh of the mussel. It was amazing: even in a place like the interior of a sunken vessel, a little blood was enough to conjure up greedy jaws from unknown hiding places. Perhaps there was a moray eel under the tub now and it was already crawling up toward me! I stuck the mussel shell hurriedly into my breast pocket and left the room. Pursued by the phantoms of my own imagination, I dashed through a long compartment, with torn planks hanging from its ceiling and got out by squeezing through a narrow window into open water again.

I heaved a sigh of relief.

That was the worst of this sort of diving gear: one is not protected by any close-fitting garments or helmet; rather one is more exposed and vulnerable than almost any fish or other denizen of the sea. I had come into contact, without noticing it, with some sort of sharp iron fittings, and little threads of blood were already welling from several long cuts on my arms and legs. I was paying for my extraordinary mobility by intensified physical risk, of which one becomes particularly aware in unfamiliar situations. Moreover, I was cut off from all communication with the world above. If anything happened to me, there would be no one to help me.

My descent had already lasted twenty minutes; it was time to swim up and fetch the camera. Mahmud and O Sheik gave obvious sighs of relief when they saw me return. I handed the spear back to them and they passed me the camera. No, I hadn't met any sea-maidens yet, I assured them. I was soon gliding down again into the glimmering blue darkness, to the ship that I now considered almost as a personal possession—as something I had won in a contest.

If I were a seaman, I could give a better description of my explorations of the vessel, from stem to stern. Its dimensions were enormous. I swam over the upper and lower decks, peered through hatches and doors into the interior, and came to an open loading hatch, through which I looked deep down into the hold and saw the massive piles of ammunition boxes. I couldn't help smiling to myself when I thought of Bill, who was perhaps, at that very moment, discussing my application with the harbor master. No, I certainly wasn't going to touch that dynamite! I should prefer the Maria Theresa thalers, unless they were locked up in inaccessible safes!

I took some photographs and made one interesting observation: just as on the coral reef, the separate species of fish here each had its own type of lair. Whenever I came across a large windlass, butterfly fish, striped black and yellow, hung over it in a shoal. Why they were so particularly fond of windlasses I couldn't make out; it may have been the numerous chinks between the machine parts, in which they could quickly hide in case of danger. The spiny-rayed perch preferred, as might have been expected, open doors and hatches, where they mounted guard in exactly the same obstinate manner, with swinging pectoral fins and inquisitive goggle-eyes, as in front of their holes in the coral reef.

I have already mentioned that the tiny, little red fish which are always seen on a coral reef pressed against the rock, here encircled the spherical masses of the steam pipes and ventilators. Certain species of parrot fish seemed to prefer the railings and companionways. Below, just above the cases of dynamite, a continuous watch was kept by two gorgeously colored emperor fish, which directed, from left to right, such suspicious glances at me that they seemed to know how dangerous the cases were that they were guarding.

It was an incomparable delight to be able to concentrate, without interference, on looking for and estimating every kind of photographic angle. If I wanted to make an upward leap of fifteen feet, I simply gave myself a little push up and there I was. If I wanted to descend thirty feet, I simply bent forward and glided down like a bird. I never got so near to third-dimensional life as I did in this wreck, where every ladder and door provoked comparison with those of a normal vessel. No bird, however cleverly it might wing its way through the rigging, could have surpassed me, for in my case gravity did not count at all. I could glide in whatever direction I chose, and I could with equal ease remain perfectly motionless in space.

I was actually standing on my head to photograph a fat, nibbling parrot fish through a tangled mass of rods when the camera suddenly jammed. I gave it a shake, but that made no difference. I looked, with suspicious misgiving, from the front of the camera through the window of the lens into the interior of the casing. Water had penetrated the cover! There was quite a lot of it too. I made a dash, as fast as I could, thrashing my fins, for the world above.

I climbed into the boat and took off the cover. A good pint of salt water streamed out of it. Part of the camera had been surrounded by water and the film had certainly been affected. I ripped it off and cleaned up the interior as well as I could with my handkerchief. Then I exposed the camera, open, to the full heat of the sun and rattled the shutter continuously for five minutes. This might make the drops inside the mechanism dry up before they could affect the gearing by rust or deposits of salt. I knew from my West Indian expedition what it meant to have to take a camera to pieces.

But after this emergency action it looked as though I had been lucky this time. The camera was functioning perfectly again. So I put in a new film, and after I had repaired the oxygen cylinder and renewed my supply of caustic soda, I glided down again to "my ship."

THE DEAD CITY

THE DEAD CITY

WE RETURNED to Port Sudan under full sail. I sat back and relaxed, deeply satisfied with the photographic fruits of my afternoon's diving. I was opening the camera when I noticed that the sliding shutter was jammed. The camera had been working quite well in the wreck, but now the two cloth slides running behind the lens were stuck. When I poked them with my finger, they started moving again. I repeated this process at least fifty times, but it did not help. It was clear that water had, after all, penetrated the mechanism and that salt and automatically forming rust were clogging the wheels. I should have to take the camera to bits as soon as possible and give it a thorough clean-up! That was not at all a pleasant prospect, for I had neither the necessary tools nor any experience whatever with the internal mechanism of a Leica.

Bill was just getting into his car when I entered the garden, followed by Mahmud. "Oh, what a bit of luck that you've turned up," he cried, visibly delighted. "We've been

95

invited to tea and I was beginning to think that I should have to go alone."

I told him what happened to the camera, prudently omitting my descent to the *Umbrea*.

"No, no, you'll have to come with me," he announced firmly. "I had to promise faithfully to bring you. We need only stay a half-hour. We'll just have tea and then I'll bring you straight back again."

I followed him with great reluctance. The problem of my camera was a leaden weight on my spirits. If I couldn't manage to repair it, I should have to cancel all my future plans. I could hardly expect to obtain a second Leica, and the Contax I used for my land photography wouldn't go into the waterproof cover.

Our host greeted us amicably and introduced me around. While I drank my tea and listened politely to the conversation, I was on tenterhooks. The talk first turned on the question whether a second billiard table ought to be bought out of club funds; that lasted a half-hour. Then the topic of the low salaries paid to government officials cropped up and the impossibility of going to France in the summer on a mere fifty pounds; that lasted another half-hour. Finally, the imminent arrival of a British destroyer was discussed and the order in which people were to sit at the ceremonial banquet in the evening was debated; that lasted a third half-hour.

The sandwiches with which I tried to console myself were so small that our hostess, to make it easier to pick them up, had stuck a toothpick in each of them. At last I couldn't stand it any longer and begged to be excused on the plea of urgent business. Bill also took his leave and drove me back.

On our way to Suakin Bill's car is held up by a herd of camels, which reluctantly allowed themselves to be jostled to the side of the road by their herdsmen. The nomadic herdsmen wore their bristled hair combed up on end.

The silhouette of Sua-
kin, the dead city, came
into view. It rose like a
weirdly crenelated castle
above the inlet of the sea
that surrounded it.

The blank and empty
façades of the ancient
palaces stood out against
the sky. Once exotic
dwelling places, now
they house only scor-
pions and bats.

Mustapha baited a three-hook line and cast it down a thousand feet. Shortly thereafter he hauled back three fine red snappers. With monotonous regularity he repeated this performance until the boat could hold no more fish.

One of Mustapha's catch. The extreme depth from which it was brought up, caused its eyes to bulge from their sockets.

I came across beds of thistle coral, with jagged points, and fluffy Alcyonaria.

Three gleaming gold dots, apparently motionless, faced the current.

In the drawing room he insisted on drinking two glasses of whisky with me, to refresh ourselves, then I rushed off to my room and, with a deep sigh, got down to work.

The hospitality dispensed at that house had been charming. But it also had a decidedly grim side! During that endless tea I had never stopped, even for a minute, thinking of those little wheels and the rust eating deeper into them.

The tools I gathered for my camera surgery were a screw driver, much too big for the job, and my pocketknife. As a measure of precaution I pulled the sheet off my bed, folded it up, and spread it over the table, which I then pushed near the window. First I unscrewed the lens. Then I loosened some ten or twelve other screws, after which the whole outer cover could be lifted off and far more parts became detached than I had expected. I ranged them all beautifully in rank and file and noted how each fitted to each. A few screws more, and then I had the actual gearing in my hand.

Quite a lot of water had gotten in. I cleaned the little wheels as well as I could with the corner of my handkerchief and a needle. To take them further apart did not seem advisable. The next thing I wanted was oil. I called Achmed. He paid close attention to what I showed him and disappeared. Shortly afterward he returned with my slippers, which I had left downstairs in the drawing room. I made him come close to the table, showed him the gearing and worked it backward and forward under his nose. Ah, now he understood. He dashed away and came back with a huge pair of pliers.

There was nothing more to do but go to the kitchen myself. The cook and all four of the staff watched me with reverent awe while I rummaged among the boxes. I couldn't find any lubricating oil, but there was plenty of good salad oil, which would do just as well at a pinch.

In the meantime, a little screw had vanished. Either the draft had blown it off the table when I opened the door, or else the steadily turning propeller in the ceiling had sent it flying. I shut all the doors and turned off the ventilator. It was a puzzle to guess where that little screw could have rolled to. It was not under the table, and I couldn't see it either under the box or under the bed.

The floor was partly covered by a rather worn carpet, which offered first-rate hiding places to a tiny screw. There were also numerous grooves in the wood of the floor, from which, during an extensive exploration, I extracted all sorts of extraordinary objects, but unfortunately not the screw I was looking for. I dragged the bed-table lamp under the bed. There was an explosion and a flash of light—and the room was plunged into darkness. Achmed appeared again in answer to my shouts. When he saw what the trouble was, he vanished and came back again with a candle. Soon after that the short circuit was fixed and the light came on again.

Meanwhile, I had begun to suspect that the screw might have managed to crawl into the camera somewhere. And that's what had happened! I gave the camera a good shake and out fell the screw onto the white sheet, looking quite ashamed of itself. Then the door opened once more and Achmed appeared. I understood from his gestures that it was dinnertime; the other guests had already assembled.

With a deep sigh I put the screw down among the rest, so that they were all in their right order and only needed to be connected up again. Then I rushed into my evening clothes, which lay ready for me. Downstairs in the drawing room a gay company had gathered and was being plied with whisky. Bill, who was in the best of tempers, introduced me and told the seal story. As the harbor master was present, I made a start by talking to his wife. Bill had already spoken to him about my wishes, but the good man had not yet made up his mind on the subject. Consequently, I exerted myself in the interests of a suitable intercession, for I positively had to have that permission. Otherwise my lovely pictures would be doomed never to be published.

Bill came over to us and asked after my camera. He had a wonderful way of keeping everything disagreeable at arm's length, with masterful optimism.

"No, no, that'll turn out all right, don't you worry," he told me soothingly. "Anyhow, I'll be free the day after to-morrow, and I've already arranged for us to drive to Suakin tomorrow at midday. The reefs there will certainly interest you and the fishing is first-rate, too."

"Oh, you'll love that!" cried the harbor master's wife. "It's only the bats that are so horrible. And there are some awful fish that keep splashing about all night long just under the terrace. But probably you'll like them!" She laughed heartily.

"We shall sleep at the hostel," Bill went on. "It's much more comfortable and cool there than it is in Port Sudan. People sleep on a big terrace overlooking the water. The fish that splash about in the night are big rays. There are masses of them in the lagoon. There's a giant jewfish to be caught there, too—"

"And hundreds of horrible bats that get into one's hair and sit on one's face in the middle of the night," the harbor master's wife interjected.

In this case I was thoroughly amenable to Bill's idea. The dead city of Suakin had been item one on my program for the journey. An important illustrated paper had expressly charged me on no account to miss visiting Suakin; it was more than ten years, they said, since any photographs had been taken there. And what particularly interested me about the city was that its decline had been due to coral reefs.

Meanwhile, Achmed had thrown open the door, and we made a move into the gaily decorated dining room. Our cook had celebrated this special occasion by exerting himself a little more than usual. We had turtle soup, fried fish, roast mutton with several vegetables and salad, followed by an excellent but somewhat overbaked pudding—apologized for by Bill as due to his unwedded state—and finally by dates, coffee, and several liqueurs, which went round the table in rotation.

At last the ladies rose and went into the drawing room, while the gentlemen went out into the garden. I took this opportunity to excuse myself and returned to my theater of war with the camera. An hour later, after a number of unsuccessful attempts, I had put it properly together again. I had five screws left over, but the camera was now working again splendidly.

Through the open window I heard the guests taking their leave and driving away. Then Bill came up to my room. He seemed in a melancholy mood and asked me whether I thought life was really worth living. I gave him as reassuring an answer as I could, then I dropped into bed, dead tired, and fell into a dreamless sleep.

Another day dawned! I could hear through the window

the confused voices of the Fuzzy-Wuzzies on their usual morning pilgrimage past the house to the harbor, where they were employed as stevedores. I went into the garden and joined Bill in his flower inspection. When Mahmud arrived, I informed him, Bill acting as my interpreter, that I would not be needing his services again till the day after to-morrow.

Mahmud took advantage of the opportunity to make a speech, in flowery language, to the Commissioner.

"What did he want?" I asked, as soon as he had gone.

Bill smiled. "To cut a long story short, it was all an elaboration of the statement that he and His Highness, the guest, were already practically brothers. He was prepared, he said, to protect you, to the last drop of his blood, against all the fearful perils of the deep. He said he was the most de-voted of my sons. And that I assuredly could not refuse a son the trifling request for a license to sell fish."

"Is such a license difficult to get?"

"Yes, it is, rather. He's been worrying me about it for two years. He wants to be allowed to sell fish direct to the ships, which would be a profitable business, of course."

"And isn't it practicable?"

"It may be. Mahmud is an awful rascal and the harbor master simply won't hear of it. Nevertheless, I'd like to help the chap. He's the best fisherman in the place, there's no doubt about that."

We had breakfast, then Bill drove to his office, and I had until two o'clock to get ready. The most important thing was to obtain a fresh supply for my oxygen cylinders: we had already telephoned, in this connection, to the Shell Works at the other end of the harbor, and the manager had consented to let me tap the firm's big containers for this purpose. As soon as the car, which Bill had put at my disposal, came back from Government House, I got Achmed to drive me over.

After going a short distance, we suddenly stopped. Achmed got out and carefully adjusted two cloth covers over the English and Egyptian pennants. It had occurred to him that this was not an official drive. After this, we went on our way.

The Shell Works were situated on the further side of a strip of desert where salt was extracted from shallow tanks connected with the sea. The manager himself conducted me through the long workshops and showed me the presses that made cans for the imported oil. This was the place, then, where the process began that ended with the rusty-tin walls of the suburban hovels! A foreman verified, with a manometer, that one of the big oxygen containers still registered atmospheric pressure of 180. That was just what I wanted. As I had brought a coupling with me from Vienna that just fitted the English thread, my cylinders were filled up in a few minutes.

Meanwhile, the bottle of developer had cooled off sufficiently in Bill's refrigerator. As soon as I returned I transformed the bathroom into a photographer's darkroom. Shortly afterward I examined my first two films. They had come out well. All the same, I resolved to postpone development of the rest until I returned to Vienna. I could cool off the developer and the sodium hydroxide fixing salt to $65°$ here all right, but not the rinsing water, and this, even after hardening, would affect the fineness of grain in the film. As I now knew how the filters worked and that I had judged

the light correctly, I could go ahead with my photography
in confidence.

Bill returned from the office in a somewhat overheated
condition. His appearance showed clearly that something
had upset him. We finished the remains of yesterday's mutton in silence. Then everything was loaded into the car, and
the staff received their final instructions.

We were just about to drive off when Bill remembered a
special fishhook which he simply had to take. The whole
house was searched, but the hook had disappeared. Achmed
ransacked the fishing-tackle chest again and again, but to no
purpose. Bill's pent-up rage burst forth in a volcanic stream.
Achmed and the rest of the staff, preserving assiduous and
zealous attitudes, kept out of his reach. With his reddened
face and rumpled hair Bill resembled an antique, symbolic
figure of "Wrath."

A little later we drove off, with Bill again in the best of
tempers. The fishhook had, after all, been found. We soon
left the town behind us and drove past the airfield into the
apparently boundless desert that stretched ahead along the
seashore. In this area it was overgrown with shrubs as tall
as a man. I noticed particularly their thick green leaves and
spherical, Chinese-lanternlike fruit.

"Those are Sodom apples," Bill told me. "They are extraordinarily poisonous. The fruits contain silky seed capillaries,
which form the vegetable silk that people use to stuff their
cushions."

Though the road was a very bad one, we drove remarkably fast in the well-sprung auto. We passed a police station.
A few miles further on Bill suddenly braked. A herd of

more than a hundred camels was blocking our way. It was only with reluctance that they began to jostle to the side of the road as we approached. One of the older animals wouldn't move till we had practically touched it with our bumper. Then it executed a high, panic-stricken leap and dashed off at an absurd gallop, rising and falling as it went like a ship in a storm. In the middle of the desert we came across a nomad, carrying a long sword tucked behind his back. He was tramping along in utter solitude.

"I had to survey a district at one time," Bill told me, "where two tribes of nomads were roaming about. I lived on the back of a camel for months. I never quite knew where the fellows were. According to the time of year, they go wherever they can find a little grass for their herds."

"Are they Mohammedans, too?"

"Yes, but they don't take their religion very seriously. They are said, and quite rightly, to be immoral."

"Oh?"

"Yes, they're a rum little lot. Adultery is common among them. Then they slash away at each other with their swords. But they don't do it so much out of fury and jealousy as on account of the compensation for damages legally collectible by a betrayed husband. Adultery has to be proved, however, beyond dispute. For that reason any Fuzzy that catches his wife with another man gives him a slash with his sword right away; then the one that is charged can't lie about it and must pay the fine."

Bill began to tell me about the highest-ranking Fuzzy of all, the *Omda,* whom he described as a dear old gentleman.

"I'm as fond of the Fuzzies as if they were my children," Bill said. "And I was really in despair when they staged a rebellion against me two years ago. I've been in quite a lot of their battles, you know. Wherever a difference of opinion breaks out, the natives go for one another at once with their swords, and then we've got to try and bring the crazy devils to their senses. And that's not too easy, for they won't listen to reason."

"An actual rebellion?" I asked.

"Yes. It was two years ago. I had locked up three religious fanatics who had defied the authorities, and the people were demanding their release. Well, I was ready to let them out, but only on condition that the rioters disperse. A crowd turned up in front of the prison, and I gave them a friendly talking-to."

"In Arabic?"

"No, in Fuzzy-Wuzzy. That's quite a separate dialect. But I couldn't do anything with them. They made a rush at me, waving their swords, with the women behind them throwing stones. It wasn't long before I was cut and bleeding; so I ordered the guard to fire. There were six killed. When I came back into the house, I found that two people had just stopped in for a whisky. I sat down and cried. After twenty years of my taking care of them!

"The affair was, of course, much criticized in Khartoum. I had given the guard orders to aim only at their legs, but the fellows had gotten trigger-happy, and so six were killed. The shooting was heard in Port Sudan, but no one took much notice of it."

I held the steering wheel while Bill lit a cigarette. The monotonous desert streamed past us, right and left. The bushes with the Sodom apples were behind us now; there was nothing to be seen but scanty undergrowth. Then we saw a doom palm standing alone on the plain. Further on lay the rusted wreck of a steamer, on the dry land of the coast. At one time the whole shore here had been under water, the waves flowing right up to the foothills of the ranges. This ten-mile-wide strip of desert had originated in the steadily increasing growth of the coral reefs, which gradually became land. The Red Sea is slowly contracting on both sides, exactly as though Asia and Africa wanted to shake hands on a wide front in this neighborhood.

At a number of places in the brown wilderness we could see irregular patches, with a bloom of delicate green upon them. The single downpour on the night of my arrival had been enough to cause grass to sprout. According to Bill, the whole desert would be green in a few weeks. We were just at the beginning of the short rainy season in this part of the world. In some years not a single drop of rain fell, but sometimes downpours of tropical abundance were experienced.

As we approached Suakin, after one-and-a-half hours on the road, we passed some Fuzzy-Wuzzies who seemed to be sowing among the low-growing bushes.

"Those are the only crops these chaps know about," Bill explained. "Whenever they see a cloud or two, they rush out to throw a few grains of wheat into the desert. When it really does rain the stalks grow up fast and are pulled up by hand."

At some distance from these strange sowers, who still wore their swords buckled across their backs as they labored at their task, we noticed a primitive tent a little to one side of the road. It was made of skins and branches. Two women, one old and one young, squatted beside it. Both were swathed in garments of purple cloth. When they saw us, they swiftly drew a fold of the material over their faces.

Meanwhile, the silhouette of Suakin had come into view. It rose like a weirdly crenelated castle above the silvery inlet of the sea that surrounded it. A conspicuous feature was a tower of considerable height, which stood some little distance from the town in the form of an obelisk, narrowing as it rose higher from the desert.

"Is that a monument of some kind?" I inquired.

"No, there's nothing romantic about it," Bill answered. "It is the chimney of an old distillery that fell into ruins long ago. That chimney is all that is left of it. It's a terrific height and you can climb a ladder inside right to the top. The construction is so massive that it will probably be still standing when the whole of Suakin, like ancient Troy, has disappeared into the sand."

We came to a settlement consisting of unpretentious, stone-built houses and primitive shacks. This was where, according to Bill, the last remaining inhabitants of Suakin lived.

"Fifty years ago the town still had a population of thirty thousand," he said. "Today there are barely three thousand left, and they have abandoned the island to settle on the mainland here."

"So the city is quite deserted now?"

"Yes, practically. There are still a few people living in eight or ten houses, but apart from them the island is wholly cut off from the rest of the country. Even our porter at the Rest-House sleeps at night on the mainland. Nothing could induce him to stay on the island after nightfall."

And Bill laughed, "If we were to be found dead tomor-

row morning, with our throats cut, no one in the neighborhood would be in the least surprised."

We turned left at the main square of the settlement and
came to a wide stone bridge leading to the island. The dead
city lay enclosed on all sides by lagoons, the latter being
connected with the sea by a channel considerably narrower
than the entrance to the harbor at Port Sudan; the channel
was very tortuous and not less than a mile long. Moreover,
so many coral reefs had grown up in front of it that it was
long since ships of any size had been able to get in. That
was why the city had been ruined.

Soon after Suakin had become a British Protectorate at
the end of the nineteenth century, the government decided
to construct a new harbor at a convenient place further
north, hence Port Sudan. By 1910 the seat of government
had already been transferred thither, and by 1924 all the important industries had followed. Since that time Suakin
has been isolated and is decaying year by year. The old
city gate at the opposite end of the bridge still stands, but
the town walls have been pulled down and their stone carried away for house construction in Port Sudan.

We drove through the gate into the ruined city. The
blank and empty frontages of the ancient palaces stood out
against the evening sky. Some were still being maintained,
with their windows and doorways boarded up. Most had
already collapsed or been left with only three or four stories
of frontage, adorned with spiral scrolls; but their former
grandeur was still clearly traceable.

Once these palaces had glittered as white as snow; their
carved woodwork had been painted green and red. At times
of festival they had been decorated with brightly colored

cloths. Seamen frequented the thronged streets; merchants came from all parts of the world; and often some great lord arrived, with a numerous retinue. On these occasions inquisitively gleaming black eyes would peep from the closely barred windows of the harems. At sunset everyone in the streets, whether rich or poor, knelt down, arms lifted to the east, foreheads bowed to the very dust. On all sides, between the gables of the palaces, glowed the variegated sails of the merchant vessels moored at the quays. High up on the tower of the mosque, that now stands lonely and neglected, the muezzin paced round, calling the faithful, far and wide, to prayer. And in breathless chambers underground lay hoarded treasure, or desperate prisoners awaiting a cruel death.

Now there was no human being to be seen in this ruined city. Vultures circled above the crumbling walls. The light of the setting sun flickered about the lofty pinnacles.

We stopped in front of a large, castlelike building with battlemented walls. To right and left of the tall wooden gate, which an old man opened for us, rusty cannon were posted. At one time this had been the National Bank of Suakin. It was now the Rest-House, the only building still kept in repair by the government. It served as accommodation for traveling officials or, as Bill remarked, for newly married couples from Khartoum, if they were not too timid to stand it. Aside from the superstitions connected with it, the Rest-House was an otherwise suitable resort for honeymooners.

We crossed a small forecourt and ascended a double staircase to the lofty rooms of the interior; here the walls were hung with ancient weapons. We deposited our luggage in the outer room that stood at a corner of the building. It was furnished with a large table, a bench, and a small desk. On the walls hung portraits of governors and drawings by former travelers. In each of two corners stood the toothed blade of a sawfish. On a wooden shelf, which extended all around the room, there was a collection of mystery stories and books on politics and fishing. The adjoining apartment was fitted up as a dining room with an ordinary table and a sideboard. Then came the bedrooms. The main reception hall was a covered wooden terrace, the whole of one side open to the water, with several camp beds scattered about and a round table placed amidst them. Here one could eat while enjoying a view of the lagoon.

Our staff, which had followed us in a second car, divided, some busying themselves in the kitchen and others making our beds for the night. One of the servants, in much confusion, reported that someone had forgotten part of the bedding. The consequence of this report was another thundering rage from Bill. I moved discreetly away and began to watch some big mackerel which had formed a hunting party right under the walls of the terrace, against the jetty.

Every one of them weighed a good fifteen or twenty pounds. There were six of them, and they appeared suddenly in the shallow water and then vanished once more into the green, obscure depths of the lagoon. They had designs upon a shoal of small fish which had taken refuge, in a panic, among the stone fragments of the decayed wall of the jetty. The mackerel would make a sudden charge upon them, with such violent impetuosity that in the course of it they leaped right out of the water, over the rocks. A silver wave of madly fleeing, leaping fish swept along the wall ahead of them.

Then, suddenly, all was still again. The survivors gathered to await the next assault.

Meanwhile, hostilities in the house had died down and we were served with a belated tea on the terrace. The staff was in a hurry to get dinner ready, so that they could return to the mainland before nightfall. I walked along the jetty with Bill. Then we sat on the terrace by the light of a large oil lamp, in comfortable basket chairs, motionless in the utter silence, which was broken only occasionally by the whirring of wings and the soft squeaking of a bat.

"Shall I tell you the story of the origin of this city?" Bill asked me. He sipped his whisky and leaned back.

"There are a good many versions, naturally, but the best is about the seven virgins presented by the King of Abyssinia [Ethiopia] to the King of Egypt. Both the monarchs were then on good terms with each other. In order that nothing might happen to the valuable consignment, the seven beauties were accompanied by a reliable eunuch. One of the nights of the journey was passed here, on this island.

"When the King of Egypt received his present he found that none of the seven was still what she should have been. The eunuch solemnly swore that no human being had been responsible. Seven of the island spirits had taken conjugal possession of the beauties by night. The King made no further protest. He sent the seven, duly provided with food and clothing, back to the island. The children born of their union with the seven spirits were the ancestors of the natives of Suakin. *Sava Ginn* means 'The spirits did it.' Hence the name Suakin."

Rays could be clearly heard splashing in the lagoon. It

sounded as though they were jumping high in the air and then letting themselves fall flat on the water. I tried to see them at it, but could distinguish nothing in the darkness.

"According to another version, Solomon built a prison here, at the end of the world. It was here, they say, that the Queen of Sheba came to visit him. At any rate Suakin was already known during the Sixth Dynasty of Egypt. The first Roman author to write an account of the city described the inhabitants as a mixture of apes and Negroes; they had no head and their eyes and mouths were situated in the chest. Trade was carried on with India and even with China. In the sixteenth century Suakin fell under Turkish dominion. Then we took the place over, and today we and the Turks are the only two nations that remain."

The moon rose slowly over the ruins. Bill went and fetched a mystery story and stretched out on one of the camp beds. For a time I turned the pages of an old chronicle which I had found in the drawer of the little desk. When the moon rose higher and the ruins were bathed in a ghostly-white light, I went for a walk through the dead city.

Hundreds of bats were wheeling about everywhere. I was startled when a stone near my feet, on the quay, scuttled away. It was a crab which came to a halt just as suddenly and stretched out two enormous claws toward me. Then, making a sudden decision, it jumped into the water, which gleamed briefly. The sea was full of innumerable phosphorescent organisms! When I threw a stone into the water, there was a flash, like that of a striking bomb, and I could clearly trace its illuminated path into the depths.

I suddenly heard peculiar sounds behind me. They came straight from the dead city and consisted of indistinct calls and shouts. I plucked up courage and went in that direction.

I picked my way over great heaps of debris. Many of the former houses were now nothing but massive piles of rubble. Then I came to a maze of narrow, tortuous lanes and had to cross a number of dark courtyards. The window openings in the tall façades, with the moon behind them, seemed to be watching my tour. From a boarded-up partition between two houses I saw light coming through the chinks in the planking.

Stealthily, without a sound, I drew nearer. I put my eye to a narrow crevice. In the flickering light of an open fire an old woman was standing, holding some kind of dark object in her hand. Near her, partially covered, lay a younger woman, undressed. The crone disappeared, mumbling to herself, and shortly afterward I began to hear groaning, whimpering sighs from the younger woman. Nothing further happened, so I stole away. The strange sounds had again grown louder. I kept thinking I should find their origin at the next building, but they stayed ahead of me like a will-o'-the-wisp.

At last I found I had walked right across the entire city. I came out onto the quay again near the city gate. The sounds had now become perfectly loud and distinct. They rose from the settlement on the mainland. Lights and shadows were darting to and fro on the wall of one of the houses there. It took a few minutes for me to realize that a sound film was being shown—an American cowboy picture in fact, dubbed in Arabic! I walked a little way over the bridge and saw hundreds of white-robed figures squatting on the ground in front of the wall of the house. I had heard the hoarse shrieks of the inadequate sound track right across the whole of the dead city!

Next morning I told Bill about the two women I had watched through the chink in the wall.

"We don't worry much about what the natives are up to," he said as we were descending, with our equipment, the broad, dilapidated stone steps that led to the jetty, where a sailboat already awaited us. "It may have been some kind of medical treatment. Cauterization is the universal cure for everything here. If someone has a stomach-ache or a sprained ankle or whatever it is, they burn a hole in him somewhere. You can give them hundreds of drugs, but they won't take a single one; they prefer to stick to their traditional methods. I'm only glad you didn't make yourself conspicuous. There might have been a frightful scandal if you had."

The felucca was a bit smaller than the one in Port Sudan. Mustapha, the owner, with whom Bill shook hands cordially, was a Fuzzy-Wuzzy of exceptionally self-confident demeanor. I could hardly believe Bill when he told me that the fellow was actually seventy years old. His face, arms, and legs were those of a healthy man of forty or forty-five. I was also struck by the robust physique and bright, intelligent eyes of some children who had come to see us off and stood round, poking their noses into everything.

The deck of the felucca was loaded with stones the size of a fist. I was soon to discover the meaning of this precaution. Mustapha had only agreed to take us on condition that he would be allowed to do some fishing on his own account, over a bank in the locality. This was precisely the time at which the first batches of pilgrims from the interior of the

Sudan arrived at Suakin and were kept at the quarantine station, under examination, for several weeks before being permitted to go on to Mecca. These few weeks represented the only chance the fishermen of Suakin had to sell their catches for decent prices.

"We often have three thousand people here," Bill said. "Many of them have tramped the whole long way from West Africa. A man may start as a bachelor, marry, do some work somewhere, and turn up in Suakin with two or three children."

"And what happens afterward? Do they travel all the way home again?"

"Some of them do, but many stay on here. Some day when you have time I'll drive you to the West African Village in Port Sudan. You could really suppose yourself in West Africa there."

The slender craft flew over the waves before the strong morning breeze. As soon as we had reached the open sea, we turned half-right. We held this course without deviation for one-and-a-half hours, further and further into the open sea. At last we arrived at our destination and Mustapha hauled down the sail. As Bill had hitherto only caught two small fish, he was not very satisfied with this preliminary jaunt.

"And I can't say a word about it," he growled. "For if I ordered him to sail further on, he'd charge me the price of what he otherwise might, conceivably, have caught. Well, we shall have to see."

Two other boats were here and ready for work. Mustapha produced a big roll of thick fishing line and baited each of its three hooks with a sardine. He then placed this bait between two stones and wound line around it so that it formed a firmly bound weight. Then he made a sling out of fishing line, in which he placed the weight, stuck a sardine through the middle of the bundle, and then let it all sink down into the depths.

And the line went down not less than a thousand feet!

After practically the whole line had run out and the weight had touched bottom, he gave it a short pull, drew in a little of the line, gave it a couple of sharp jerks, and then started hauling the line in again at a rapid rate.

When, after a considerable time, the end came in sight, each of the three hooks had a fine red snapper hanging to it! As the fish had been brought up from such exceptional depths, the reduced pressure had caused their eyes to bulge from their sockets. Mustapha, with perfect tranquillity, detached them from the hooks and repeated the former procedure.

I gradually realized what happened under water. When Mustapha gave the first jerk, he was shaking off the sardine he had stuck in the sling; the sling then came untied and the length of line that held the two stones together loosened and came off. That was why he had pulled the line in a little. The stones then fell off and the bait came loose. The fish immediately dashed at it, and Mustapha, with a few dexterous jerks, got them onto the hooks. This performance was repeated with monotonous regularity. The hooks hardly ever came up empty. There must have been a pretty closely packed crowd of fish down there.

The sun rose higher and higher. Bill and I looked on dejectedly as the stones in the bottom of the boat grew fewer and fewer and were continually replaced by fat red fish. We had to change location twice because sharks appeared and seized the fish halfway up to the surface. Bill, interpreting for Mustapha, told me the fish only came once a year to this bank. Most obligingly, they did so at the very time when the pilgrims arrived. Allah had indeed arranged this matter very well.

If there had been a reef anywhere about, I should have asked to be dropped there while this was going on; but we were right out in the open sea, so there was nothing to do but wait. Finally, the last stone was used up and Mustapha set sail again. Bill was so annoyed over a touch of the sun he had caught from this business that he let his spinning bait drift in the water without paying any attention to it. Then came a jerk, and everything went topsy-turvy. With a shrill squeal, the line ran out from the reel and the rod bent till I thought it would break. Bill was now again quite in his element. He cursed and snorted, abused Mustapha for not taking in sail quickly enough and me for sitting on the wrong side of the boat.

"There, there," he yelled. I racked my brains to guess what he meant.

"What is it? What do you want me to do?"

"There, it's there, look, man! That thing. There's what I want!"

The line squealed again and the fish dashed frantically off in a fresh tantrum.

"If I only knew what you were talking about!"

"Ah, damnation—right, right, right!"

At last I had discovered that he meant the fish gig or spear, which was buried deep under the heap of red fish. Everything in the boat had been made slippery by those infernal fish. Wherever you went, you fell over them!

Finally the fish was pulled in near enough for us to see it. It was a magnificent barracuda. Just as we had him close to the boat, he suddenly leaped into the air, with a violent shudder. Flashing and sparkling, he dropped back into the water.

"If only I don't lose him! Oh, if only I don't lose him!" groaned Bill, sweating at every pore with his efforts. The fish, tiring, was only offering slight resistance now. Mustapha had seized the barbed iron gig and lunged into the water with it at the fish. But he missed.

"Get him! Get him, man!" yelled Bill, beside himself with excitement.

Then came the catastrophe. The fish flung itself into the air with a second mighty toss, grazed the side of the boat—and the line hung loose in the water!

The fish had managed to break free at the last moment, taking with him, too, the spoon bait—the very one we had been looking for so strenuously at the time we started! Bill, foiled, rummaged for his cigarettes.

"Idiot of a fellow!" he snorted, not deigning to give the unfortunate Mustapha a second glance. "And my best spoon, of course! Cost me twelve and six [about $1.75]. It might be three months before I find another like it. Damn, damn, damn, damn!"

We sailed on in silence till we reached the reefs opposite the entrance to the harbor again. As I was about to take to the water there, Mustapha made the gestures with which Mahmud had already familiarized me. He meant that the tiger sharks living thereabouts were particularly ferocious and bigger than our boat itself.

I dived. So these were the murderous reefs that had destroyed Suakin! They certainly looked gloomy enough. The water was rather turbid. I could only see thirty feet ahead at most. I glided across a steep gradient, most of which was composed of dead coral rock. I swam as fast as I could to the bottom and squatted down on a rock there.

Out of the impenetrable darkness swarmed some hundreds of gorgeously gleaming gold dots. They streamed past me in a long procession like a flock of sheep. Then five large pompanos, with a bloom of gold upon them showed up, surrounded me, and then disappeared again. Two clumsy-looking fish of gigantic size, with broad heads and thick lips, arrived some distance below me and stared up at me. Suddenly fish at least twice as big as any of the rest turned up. They were so curiously shaped that at first I took them for a mere figment of my imagination. As they were swimming at the extreme limit of my vision, I could only see their bare outlines. Then they came closer.

Their squat figures were characterized by an unpleasantly protuberant blue swelling on the front of the head. Each must have weighed forty or sixty pounds. There were eight or ten of them. Soon they turned round and came straight at me. Their jaws bristled with hideous yellow teeth. The expression on their faces reminded me slightly of sheep. But owing to the swelling they looked like fantastic bogies. A heavy, dull thud sent a tremor through the water. The whole shoal wheeled, panic-stricken, swam off a little way, turned back, got another fright as a second tremor ran through the water.

Twenty big pompanos now appeared, in the greatest agitation, from all sides, and surrounded me, while for the second time the long procession of gold dots came streaming past. I sat with my harpoon ready and my back pressed to the rock; I did not feel comfortable by any means. Life in this channel did not resemble anything I had seen anywhere else. And owing to the impenetrability of the dark turbid water everything had a particularly gloomy and terrifying aspect.

I was convinced that sharks were in the immediate neighborhood. If they attacked me here, my chances of survival were slender. Perhaps, too, I had been too long in the sun, for my whole body was frozen. Slowly, I made my way back to shallow water. As I couldn't take any photographs in this turbid pea soup, there was no sense in exposing myself to unknown perils.

Still, I wanted to take a prize of some kind back with me. When I saw two big eyes glaring up at me among the rocks, I lunged with the harpoon. It was a porcupine fish, which had blown itself up into a huge balloon, with extraordinarily long spines projecting from it on all sides. When Bill came to help me lift it into the boat, Mustapha stopped him, explaining that spines of this type were extremely poisonous.

I saw that Bill wanted to return. I also, to be frank, had had enough. I was not in the right frame of mind today for this particular abyss. We sailed back in subdued moody silence. At the Rest-House Bill bought two of Mustapha's innumerable fish from him; then we had a meal and drove back again to Port Sudan.

CORAL MAGIC

CORAL MAGIC

When a passenger steamer arrives at Port Sudan, a few particularly seasoned travelers, old hands in the tropics, invariably venture into the town. Protected by their sun helmets, they have themselves rowed across the harbor in one of the small boats, march over the bright, dusty tract of land, wide and shadeless, on which the Red Sea Hotel and the government building stand in solitary state, and finally come to the public park, where a blind beggar sits at the entrance, rattling off endless chapters of the Koran.

In the middle of the park they discover a Greek temple, made of plaster, which they admire or criticize according to the level of their understanding of art. Then, at the opposite end of the park, they enter the shopping quarter. By this time most of them are already suffering so much from the heat that they are hardly in a condition to obtain any substantial reduction in the prices of a pantherskin, which would probably be cheaper in England, or of the really pretty Sudanese goldsmiths' and silversmiths' work.

They hurriedly buy yet another nomad's sword, or a brightly colored Arabic bedside carpet; sip a melting ice cream at the Ramona or its neighboring competitor, the Britannia; and then feel that they have had enough, for the rest of their lives, of this town in the middle of that incubator, otherwise called the desert. Aboard their steamer again, still in the land of the living, they tell the tale of their heroic deeds.

One or two of them may have noticed, on their return journey, a structure in the shape of a horseshoe, which keeps the Red Sea Hotel and the Government House company in their burning solitude. This is the Port Sudan swimming pool. In contrast with the extremely exclusive pool at the English Club, anyone, even colored, is admitted here. The water is changed every third day with a fresh supply from the sea.

A tall old Sudanese sells the tickets and hires out bathing trunks. A second Sudanese stands behind an ice-cream counter under an awning and mixes cold drinks for those who come sweating out of the warm water. Both attendants perform their functions in slow motion. When you give them a shout, they first raise their heads, then they turn their heads, then they glance in the direction of the shout—and not until then do their weary limbs begin to move. My peculiar behavior in this pool was only just able to arouse a flicker of interest in them.

Under the attentive gaze of everyone else present at the time I lay prone at the edge of the concrete basin, held my submarine camera below the surface of the water, and put myself to the trouble of photographing a long strip of wood into which I had hammered fifteen nails.

I had been worried about the distance focusing. Owing to refraction, all distances are erroneous under water, to the extent of about a third; the exact figure of the ratio is sometimes dependent on the warmth and salt content of the water. It was perfectly possible that the refraction values given by the waters of the Mediterranean and Caribbean seas would not apply here. I had therefore hammered nails into a lath at precisely measured distances, and by photographing these nails under water, I could see on the developed film which of the nails was most clearly outlined, and therefore in focus.

The result was a somewhat altered figure, in accordance with which I converted all distances. I entered the corrected distances on a yardstick, which thenceforward I always took with me on fish-hunting expeditions with the camera.

Naturally, the fish would not wait for me to measure off distances before taking their portraits. Thus, I used the following trick: When I had a fish in front of the camera, I made a quick search in another direction for a coral which was about the same distance from me as the fish, measured the range of the coral, adjusted the camera to that range, and then photographed the fish—that is, if it was still there.

It is a better plan to take a half-hour a day swimming about the place with the yardstick and estimating distances. After a few days my eye had become so accurate that I was hardly ever off more than three inches in a yard. I carried the yardstick fastened to my shoulder with a string, so that it floated over me and was always at my disposal. I sharpened one end of it, so as to be able to use it as a weapon in case of need; for to carry the spear as well as the camera would impede my stalking maneuvers.

I had a regular program each day now. I was awakened by Achmed at seven; at eight Mahmud arrived and took my equipment to the boat; by ten we were already lying at anchor over the Wingate Reef. The weather was exceedingly favorable. In the mornings the sea remained almost perfectly smooth, with a long ground swell; the usual northerly wind did not rise until shortly before midday, and it took us back to Port Sudan in the late afternoon under full sail. Mahmud and O Sheik soon got used to my methods of work. While I swam and dived, they squatted in the boat or gossiped or else pulled the sail over their heads and slept. I saw them several times at their prayers, their bodies rising and bending in the little craft that floated in solitary state at the edge of the reef.

During these days I often had the feeling that every muscle in my body was enjoying itself on its own initiative. Wherever I dived, an endless new world lay before me. Every abyss which I explored beckoned me on to the next, which lay even deeper, even more sinister, below me. I came upon views so lovely that they took my breath away. And all my impressions took on a special spice from the fact that I was entering forbidden ground. I never allowed myself to forget that a shark might be waiting behind the next rock; I could never so lose myself in the beauty of a view as to forget to keep a sharp lookout.

A diver's greatest danger lies within himself: it is the sudden onset of fear. So long as he keeps calm and encounters hazards with full realization of all the dangers inherent in them, everything is all right. But it is fatal to allow himself to be disconcerted by some unexpected occurrence. He is then in the position of a tightrope walker who loses his balance. Up to then his hands have automatically performed all the manipulations necessary to keep the respirator and other equipment in action, but after the onset of fear they seem helpless.

Breathing becomes twice as fast. He feels he is getting too little air. He pumps in fresh in a hurry, but too much of it. He makes for the surface and has to puff to regain his balance. Meanwhile, he bumps into a rock, or cuts himself, till it burns, on a coral; he turns round, but the string holding the yardstick has gotten tied up around the respirator and the camera is thumping ominously against the oxygen cylinder. Water has pentrated the mask and he has to lie down on his back and pump air hard into the thing.

Why was it he got so excited? It may have been only some unimportant trifle. An unexpected contact behind him. At once tautly stretched nerves slacken, an incautious movement is made—and a whole series of blunders ensues. It may be possible to resume his coolness and inner equilibrium; or there may be nothing but to make a dash, with a wildly beating heart, for the surface. With the feeling that it may already be too late and he will never reach fresh air and daylight in time, at last he bursts through to the sparkling surface of the water, hurriedly turns off the mouthpiece tap, and spits out the mouthpiece, breathing in deep draughts of liberating air. Then with trembling knees he climbs up a short slope of rock, and gradually the shock subsides as he lies in the warm sun.

The very fact that I had still not yet met any fair-sized shark got on my nerves. As soon as I saw the first one, I should immediately know what I was about; I should know whether the sharks here were really of a different type, more aggressive than those I had encountered in other seas. Where the deuce had they gone to? Were they deep down somewhere or off some outlying island, assembling for their mysterious mating ceremonies, leaving only the little ones, not yet of ripe age, at home? I had seen quite a number of small sharks of that sort, some of them absurdly long and thin. But the really big ones, against which I was continually being warned, had so far only shown up in my imagination.

It also occurred to me that I should not be able to count on anyone's assistance if anything really did happen. Mahmud and O Sheik were sitting up there in the boat, and I could easily guess how they would behave if I didn't reappear after an hour. They would row round and round in desperate anxiety and look down through the waves, but they would never be able to see right down to the depths at which I usually disported myself.

From below, one's upward range of vision is much longer. I could still see, from depths of 90 and 100 feet, the silhouette of the boat lying at anchor off the edge of the reef. But if I reached a still lower submarine chasm, I could only see at most 50 or 60 feet up. The deeper I went, the grayer and grizzlier the water became. Here were missing the bright solar reflections which continuously altered all the shades of color nearer the surface. Stale and oppressive, the motionless water hemmed in my body and the coral formations about me. I felt that I had to push this inert mass of liquid out of my way. My hands, when I caught a glimpse of them, were as pallid as those of a dead man. Not the slightest glimmer of red penetrated this depth.

Thick, serrated-type groupers, speckled black, glided up before me and turned to sink back again, their forms fading

If I moved, butterfly fish (*top*) and angelfish (*bottom*) came gliding up in a panic, examined me timidly, and then scampered off like goblins. These fishes were as brightly colored as if a painter had been testing his whole palette on them.

Beside the wall of a coral reef, about fifty-five feet down, bulged the gigantic head of a brain coral, surrounded by platterlike Montipora.

In the shallow water above the plateau of the reef I caught sight of something moving in a peculiar fashion. Panther rays were performing a round dance of courtship.

Disappointed not to have gotten the shot I wanted, I heaved a sigh. Perhaps they heard me, for the larger creature, the female, doubled in its tracks and made straight for me in a diagonal drive and the smaller male came fluttering after her.

I found grottoes that ran far below the solid block of the reef, for more than 150 feet, and wildly meandering sidetracks and crossways which I followed, while ghostly pairs of eyes gleamed out from the darkness at me.

The female panther ray was right up to me now, just turning and gliding off sideways over the corals of the reef plateau. I waited till she raised her flippers—then I took the photograph!

The dreaded firefish has pectoral fins which resemble a peacock's tail and under its beautiful comb are hidden the fearful stings.

into greenish water. An enormous fish of angular shape, looking as though cut out of paper, hung motionless in the distance. Close to me a small recess had formed in the rock. So as to protect my back for a minute, I sat down in it and pulled myself together. Then a chill slowly began to rise up my legs. It was not a natural chill, for even at this depth the water was still relatively quite warm. It was a chill of uneasiness.

If there are two of you, diving is a pleasure—and fun for experts. If you are alone, you are at the mercy of your worst enemy, your own imagination. What might be approaching my recess from both sides? And what might there be in the recess itself, in the dark hole behind?

The only thing to do was to think of something else. How was the camera focused? How many photographs had I taken up to now? Was everything still watertight? I forgot the depth and the gloom and began to wonder whether I could photograph that fish that looked as if it were cut out of paper. I started swimming again. I had captured a new stronghold, for the next time I came to this neighborhood, it would already be familiar to me and the unknown would have lost its terrors.

So as to be able to recognize, later on, the separate types of coral I photographed, I broke a small piece off each stem and kept these specimens in the boat, preserved in little vials of alcohol. The form in which these pieces grew was quite distinct in each case, according to the environment. I had therefore to be able to recognize individual polyps, which varied amazingly in size: in the case of the stinging fire corals, belonging to the jellyfish family of polyps, they were only visible to the naked eye as tiny points; the star corals were about a half-inch in diameter; and the remarkable mushroom-shaped corals grew to the size of one's hand.

These mushroom corals form, it is true, an exception in every respect. While all other corals combine, like plants, with the soil beneath, the mushroom corals only do so at the very early stage of their growth. They then resemble a mushroom in the course of developing a continually widening head on its delicate stem. The polyp is carried on this head, which later breaks off and thereafter lies among the corals like a dumpling; it is picked up by the waves and tossed about; but the polyp thrives perfectly well on this treatment and grows out in all directions. The stem is also content with its fate. It at once starts developing a new head, which after a certain time, at the right moment, breaks off in its turn.

The weird thing about reef-forming corals is the fact that there seems to be absolutely no limit to their span of existence. If a stem grows too big, other grubs attach themselves to it and new colonies overgrow and displace it; but here and there one of them continues to grow and expand, regains its youth, and in its turn starts displacing the others. The oldest trees in the world have lived for some thousands of years; how many tens of thousands of years has this or that family of corals existed, growing up out of the bright maze of colors behind it? In this submarine world, there is no distinction between young and old, only an endless surge of new sprouting, which takes its building material—chalk —from the sea itself, in order to erect indestructible strongholds against that very sea.

How did the reef grow up, how did it turn into a solid wall? Up on its flat top it was hardly possible to see how the rock, worn smooth by the waves, could have been formed. But here below I could see the platelike structure was hollow underneath. Everywhere pockets and fissures led downward, creating entries to a system of grottoes which were undermining the plate of the reef from the depths. I found grottoes that ran far below the solid block of the reef for over fifty yards, and wildly meandering sidetracks and crossways which I followed underground.

Ghostly pairs of eyes gleamed out from the darkness of these grottoes. Pallid, hideous crayfish glided by like phantoms. I met cuttlefish and there were slimy halls of the sea where a beam of light fell from some lofty window and played over the walls, unveiling the structure of the reef.

While, up above, the towering stems had been built into walls by calcareous insects, fragments of coral, and tiny chalk-isolating organisms, here below the sea was nibbling away the cement again and the buried stems were reappearing. Like spirits from the other world they brandished their dead arms from the rock. Jagged points, resembling stalactites, hung from the vault. I took a closer look at them: they were the lower ends of corals growing upward. Upward . . . into the rock!

When I left these caverns of the past for daylight once more, my eyes were blinded by the dazzling brightness of the living corals, and I had again to get accustomed to distinguishing the multiplicity of details.

The bright fluttering, as of a butterfly's wing, over the bluish-violet bloom of the cluster yonder—was that caused by fish or by sunbeams which had grown heads and graceful fins? One of them drew nearer and became interested in a small crab hiding, apparently, in a nosegay. As the fish remained motionless for an instant I noticed that every scale in its body presented a different hue of the rainbow. All the colors were there. Blue, red, golden, and silver decorations and patterns traversed the graceful fins and encircled the head. He was gone! The little crab, too, had vanished. It was the old, sad story of eat and be eaten.

The myriad hues reached quite shallow water, where I was collecting, under the breaking waves, dainty little snails —the dove and Pharoah varieties. Violet and purple snake stars curled among the twigs of the flowerlike clusters. Blue-black and dark-red sea urchins seemed to be playing a crafty game with their spiteful prickles. Nile-green, azure, and orange-yellow water lilies unfolded their gorgeous, starry crowns. And in the calyxes themselves strangely tinted, shell-less snails were posted, feeding on the corals like caterpillars browsing on flower petals in a garden.

If I moved, butterfly fish came gliding up in a panic, some with a huge eye outlined on the body, which examined me timidly as they scampered off like goblins. Soft, scaleless sea jumpers glided high up on the rocks and sprang, when I chased them, like grasshoppers to the next stone. But, look out! It would be better to be very careful where I put my hand. My fingers jerked back just in time! There lay a Synanceja, the ugliest of all fish. It lay close to a coral, like a bunch of seaweed, and slowly rolled the skin back from its dorsal prickles. Its sting is said to be as painful as that of a scorpion. Sometimes it even proves fatal.

But the blue and brown surgeonfish, which swam so harmlessly and nimbly about over the flowery meadows of the sea, also carried weapons I had better steer clear of. They are so named on account of two little daggers which can be snapped open at the root of the tail—reminiscent of the lancet once applied to the veins by the barber-surgeon. On the other hand the spindly-thin filefish, weird squadrons of which ride their patrols beneath the waves, were harmless. Despite their wicked-looking, crocodile-type jaws they were timid, and when I chased them, they dashed off over the water in long leaps into the distance.

One of them had a queer look. Had he, by any chance, lost his upper jaw in a fight? No, he was a different species: a "half-beak." For some incomprehensible reason nature had denied him the upper half of his crocodilelike muzzle.

And the little creature on the rock yonder, looking like a twisted brooch? What could that be? It was staring at me with a glittering little black eye. When I moved my finger toward it, it squirmed and came to a halt a bit further off on the rock, where it kept as still as before. It was a pipefish! It is a near relation of the sea horse and looks as little like a true fish. It is also related to the Australian harlequin fish, which must be the most extraordinary creature in the seven seas. According to published drawings it resembles a brightly beribboned carnival figure and also has a pocket in its stomach for carrying its young, like a kangaroo.

If I wanted to see any more peculiar-looking shapes, all I had to do was to smash a pen coral and out came, like the residents of a hotel on fire, a number of little creatures, fleeing from their hiding places in all directions. Grotesquely patterned trapeze crabs ran races with a bright-green grasshopper-crayfish. Tiny little spotted fishes, no bigger than one's thumbnail, came floundering out of the wreckage. A date mussel, which had been living inside the coral, lay helpless, broken from its moorings. A small, reddish scale star wriggled under an iridescent annelid worm, which curled up and fled.

Even the rocks lying in the shallows were full of life. Their tops had been selected as sitting accommodations by sea squirts, moss animalcula, and sponges. When I caught hold of them, my hands were filled with numbers of little worms. They were embedded in the narrowest of crevices and channels; many had built themselves tiny houses out of sand and fragments of mussel shells; others merely used the rock as a temporary refuge and went out hunting at night. Brickred scale worms adhered to the rocks like snails, by suction; others extended slimy threads, or stung me, when I touched them.

The entire reef was nothing but a sponge of inordinate size, thronged with life. Creatures could live on it in a thousand and one ways, and they were adapted, in a thousand and one ways, to live in the fashion they did.

Out in the open sea it was different. There, living conditions were the same for most animals. Accordingly, all fish had the same purposeful torpedo outline; for in order to survive in open water they had to be fast movers; fast in the chase and fast in order to evade pursuit themselves. On the reef, however, even those clumsily built could keep going, provided that they were protected by armor, stings, poisonous discharges, or deceptive coloring.

Here the plump sea hedgehogs, which blow themselves up into a balloon in the face of danger, waddled about. They were accompanied by boxfish, the tails of which are their most movable part; by dishevelled-looking mailed cheeks, resembling a rock overgrown with weed; by grotesque triggerfish, which lock themselves in crevices with their single horns, which can be cocked to a considerable height; and last but not least by armies of coral fish, the bright coloring of which renders them as little noticeable among the corals as are flat gray plaice upon the sand.

Each of these examples of marine life, taken separately, is unique, a miracle before which one can only wonder at the fantastic whims of creation thus disclosed. If they are observed in their natural environment, much that was mysterious attains a special significance and many a queer figure's hidden meaning comes to light.

Countless reciprocities related the reef to its residents, and the latter again to one another. Basically, this whole great community resembled clockwork, in which each tiny wheel has to be studied in order to understand the rest. This clockwork, during many million years, had had a good deal of practice, and its individual wheels had adapted themselves to one another, undergone transformations and improvements, or been smashed and vanished.

The reef had developed in exactly the same way as a human city. In a city, too, there are a thousand and one ways of living, which are exploited by human beings in their vocations. Each of the latter requires a particular equipment and a special kind of adaptation, and each has its effect on the rest in the great economic machine. One trader's business expands, another's is ruined. And this was precisely what happened among the crustacea, fish, and worms of the reef. Those that were advantageously endowed spread and became important wheels in the clockwork. Those that could not adapt themselves to the given conditions were destroyed, and other wheels took their vacant places.

I looked under a rock and saw what seemed to be a wonderfully lovely flower. But it was a fish! It was the famous *Pterois volitans,* the firefish, the sting of which is no less dreaded than that of the Synanceja. Its pectoral fins had broadened into feathery formations extending all round the body in a gorgeous circle, like a peacock's tail. From the back an equally gorgeous comb bristled—concealing the dreaded stings!

I watched a shoal of fish approach and gather round this dangerous flower in a ring. When I myself drew nearer and prodded the creature with my yardstick, his terrified movements showed that he had never had such an experience before. All his splendor existed simply to warn all aggressors: Look out for yourself, don't come too near my stings! Helplessly twitching and fluttering, he was driven by the stick out into the sunlight, where I photographed him. I caught another without difficulty, by moving a couple of nets, which I had fastened to handles, toward him from left and right.

Another time I was swimming at the foot of a precipice of the reef when I saw a double movement at a considerable distance. It rose vertically up the wall of the reef and glided over its top in the shallow water. At first I thought it was two big turtles following each other, then I realized it was a couple of large panther (or spotted-eagle) rays, swimming close behind each other in an impulsive courtship.

I darted upward and saw both creatures, in quite shallow water, performing a round dance over the top of the reef, as they beat the water with their long, whip-shaped tails and speckled lateral flippers. I took a photograph, then I tried to get nearer. But at once both got on the move again and swam off so fast through the shallows that I had all I could do to keep them in sight.

Suddenly the foremost doubled like a hare and swam for the top of the reef again, its partner following closely. I tried to cut them off, but by the time I myself had gotten to the top of the reef, they were already beneath me, in deep water, swimming on in a straight line, so that they were bound to disappear from my field of vision during the next few seconds.

Perhaps they both heard my sigh of disappointment; at any rate the foremost, the somewhat larger of the pair, evidently the female, doubled in its tracks as unexpectedly as before and made straight for me in a diagonal drive, while the smaller male came fluttering hastily after her.

I took a photograph, then concentrated my whole attention on the camera. It looked as if the rays, in their amorous frenzy, would come up quite close to me; I should have to take advantage of this unique opportunity. Range I put at one meter. Exposure could stay as it was. For speed a hundredth part of a second would do. Parallax? I should have to keep the upper point of the finder a little below the center of the crosslines. Ready!

I was just in time. The foremost ray had come right up to me and was just turning and gliding off sideways over the corals of the top of the reef. I waited till she raised her flippers, and then I took the photograph. Actually, the result was twofold. On the one hand the picture, with two others, won me a gold medal later on, and on the other hand the barely audible sound of the release catch was enough to send both rays dashing off in a panic.

If I hadn't seen it myself, I wouldn't have thought it

possible that such clumsy creatures could attain such incredible speed. In their sudden fright they shot off like two great bats and it could not have been five seconds before they were swallowed up in the distance.

ENCOUNTER
WITH THE DEVIL

ENCOUNTER WITH THE DEVIL

"How is it you're not married?" I asked Bill. We were sitting in the drawing room, drinking tea. Bill was in a good humor. For a wonder, he had won his game of golf that day. Deep in his well-upholstered armchair, he was lying back, blowing a cloud of smoke into the air, and dangling a slipper from one big toe.

"Because," he answered in a deliberate tone, "the women who interested me didn't want to share the life of an English colonial official. And those who wouldn't have minded . . . well, there you are."

"Besides," he went on, "I've got Achmed, and he's trouble enough."

"Trouble? I thought he was a jewel."

"No doubt, but not always." The barometer of Bill's good humor dropped a few degrees.

"Once I heard that Achmed was ill," Bill related. "I sent for the doctor, but Achmed refused to see him. Next day I called him in to find out what the trouble was. He said,

'I'm not ill, only heartsick, and it's all your fault!' 'Why mine?' I asked. Well, it was because I had called him and then whistled for him as though he were a dog. It's not easy to have dealings with these people; they're very sensitive. One trifle puts them in a huff, another enchants them.

"Whenever I tell Achmed off about anything, he starts a flood of counterquestions: 'Do I smoke your cigarettes?' he asks. 'Do I drink your whisky or steal your sugar? Do I go to the market and get drunk? Do I seduce other men's wives? No, I am a man who reveres God and prefers to walk in the straight path of virtue.' 'Well, I'm very glad to hear it,' I reply, not knowing what else to say. And to think that I treat him like a son. He's got a wife, the third I've bought him, and when I go to England, I always send him home, miles into central Africa, at my expense. He doesn't have such a bad time of it, the rascal."

Achmed, as if he had guessed we were talking about him, had silently entered the room. He glided swiftly between us, refilled our cups, and disappeared again.

"And that incident yesterday, when you wanted to take his picture," Bill continued. "That's just another example of his unpredictable behavior."

I smiled, recalling how Achmed wouldn't pose for his picture until he had replaced his dirty turban with a fresh one. At least, I thought, he's neat, a commendable trait in a houseboy.

Bill rummaged fastidiously in the big cake basket. He always declared that cakes would be the death of him. But he was far from resenting the idea of such a death.

Suddenly he asked me. "By the way, would it interest you at all to come to Khartoum with me?"

"Khartoum? When?"

"In two-and-a-half weeks. A big reception will be given by the Governor-General of the Anglo-Egyptian Sudan to celebrate the King's birthday. All the Sudanese chiefs and high dignitaries will be there. I shall have to attend too and could easily get you an invitation."

"How will you get there?"

"We shall take a sleeper on the train, which takes two days and a night, and come back by plane. I am sure it will be well worth your while. You will be introduced to His Excellency, and we shall pay a visit to Sir Sayed Abdel Rahman, the Mahdi Pasha, who is the religious head of the Sudan. A ball will also be given."

"Ah—"

When evening drew near, Bill always became the personification of the "Spirit of Enterprise." In the mornings, when he attended to his flowers, his mood was middling. But when the sun rose higher and the time for him to go on duty approached, his spirits flagged considerably. Sometimes he did not say a single word at lunch. At tea, however, with anticipation of the evening ahead his good humor usually returned. It wasn't quite the same in my case, for Bill had a program for nearly every evening which lasted at least until midnight.

Bill laughed. "Are all the Viennese the same as you? I imagined them to be quite different!"

"Of course they are," I replied. "Especially when they've been swimming in the sea all day long."

"Well, you've still time to think it over," Bill went on. "Today you'll be meeting a few colleagues of your own. We are going first to have a drink with the Port Manager, and then we shall dine together aboard the torpedo boat that came in today. According to what the captain told me, all his officers are enthusiastic divers. I understand they went down off Malta and in the Gulf of Aqaba, where the ship has been stationed for the last few weeks."

That was interesting. I had been racking my brains for days to think of someone near here who might be able to dive with me. I needed, for photographic purposes, a man I could use as a standard of comparison with the corals. If I never photographed anything but corals and fish, no one could ever guess their size from the pictures.

"How long will the ship be here?"

"Four or five days, I think."

We went upstairs to our rooms and I could hear Bill having his bath, midst a tremendous splashing and uproar. Then I heard him singing and gargling, and soon after he reappeared in white evening dress, freshly shaved and sprinkled with Eau de Cologne, like a youthful Adonis.

At the house of the Port Manager, where a number of guests were already sitting in a circle, with glasses of whisky in their hands, I was given a seat next to a lady who was a passenger on a Swedish steamer that was passing through. I was told that she spoke German and that we should therefore be able to have a heart-to-heart talk in our mother tongue.

"I hear you come from Sweden, madam, and will only be here for a few days on your way through," I began politely.

"*O ja-a-a!*" came the answer, with an amicable nod.

"Did you travel direct, or break your journey in Italy?"

The next day following a heavy rain I visited the West African Village in Port Sudan. In contrast with the town proper, here I found high mud walls with circular kraals behind them, topped by conical roofs of straw.

A young Negro woman, in spite of the censorious glances from the male population, allowed me to photograph her face.

The shoal, with its hundreds of inquisitive eyes, approached me.

"Girsch kabir!" the men shouted excitedly. I looked where they were pointing and saw two fins, racing about in a playful fashion. Odd, I thought, that they should remain the same distance apart. Probably two sharks performing some sort of mating rite.

I was overboard in a trice, determined to observe this curious situation.

Any fish may be greedily seized by the dangerous tentacles of the giant sea anemone.....

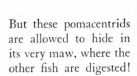

But these pomacentrids are allowed to hide in its very maw, where the other fish are digested!

She nodded. *"O ja-a-a! O ja-a-a!"*

Obviously she had not understood me.

"Is your boat bound for India or Johannesburg?"

She nodded again in the friendliest way. *"O ja-a-a! O ja-a-a!"*

It was clear that she spoke only Swedish, not a single word of German. Bill, with the best of intentions, had gotten it all wrong. When I told him, later on, what a peculiar conversation I had had, he nearly split his sides with laughter. He, at first, had been sitting next to her, and she had then replied nothing but "O ye-e-es! O ye-e-es!" to everything he said. After that, in order to get rid of her, he had handed her over to me.

Aboard the torpedo boat the deck was gaily beflagged. We were served with cocktails even stronger than the usual whisky we drank. The officers talked animatedly with a number of ladies in long evening dresses. After the officers had been introduced to me, they showed me their diving helmets and also the breathing apparatus so much used in the Mediterranean. They had shot a few fish off Malta, but had not done any diving in the Gulf of Aqaba, for there were sharks in that neighborhood.

I turned to one of the officers who looked particularly big and strong and asked him whether he would care to come over to the reefs with me one day. I told him how magnificent it was out there, that there was no danger, and that I needed someone to help me so that my photographs would show a standard of size to compare with the corals.

"Standard of size?" A man with bushy eyebrows joined us. It was the captain. "No, we can't have His Majesty's officers eaten by sharks for that purpose!"

"But there are hardly any sharks in that neighborhood!"

"Hardly any, eh? Well, 'hardly any' is enough for us."

"Didn't you ever hear that we've an exceptionally good swimmer in Port Sudan?" asked one of the ladies, turning to me. "He would be just the man you want!"

After the official banquet, when we had all driven to the English Club, where dancing was going on in the light of Chinese lanterns, Bill introduced me to a young man sitting at the next table. It was the swimmer. He had fair hair and a broad, cheerful countenance.

His wife happened to be dancing at the time, so we talked undisturbed. I told him how wonderful the reefs were, and in a very short time he was all agog to go. We arranged that he should accompany me the following Sunday.

The dance ended and the swimmer's wife returned. She was very slender and very pretty. Her smile faded a little when she heard what we intended to do.

"Oh, what a pity," she said. "Unfortunately, my husband is already booked for next Sunday."

"What about the Sunday after?" I asked quickly.

"We're already booked up for that, too," was the firm reply. I invited her to dance and asked her whether the idea was really out of the question. Unfortunately, it was. She was quite certain on that point.

"You must promise me," she said, "that you won't make any further attempts to put such silly notions into my husband's head."

"Why not? Nothing's in the least likely to happen to him!"

"Why not? Well, if you must know, I'll tell you. It took him three years to make up his mind to marry me," she said laughingly, "and I'm not going to let him run any risks now."

The many couples moving rhythmically to the music under the Chinese lanterns made a pretty picture. Bill outdid everyone else on the floor. Performing rumba steps that would have done honor to Fred Astaire, he swung the ladies round in the most ingenious pirouettes. During a brief interval he informed me that a Mr. Row, the Port Sudan diver, was sitting at a table on the other side of the room. I really would have to meet him.

"I was telling him about you a little while ago and he didn't believe a word I said. It'll certainly amuse you to have a chat with him."

We went across the room together and Bill introduced me. Mr. Row was a little, thickset fellow, with a large, practically empty beer glass on the table before him.

"Oh, so you're the famous diver," he observed, with engaging candor. "The last time I saw Mr. Clark, I told him I didn't believe a word of your stories."

Bill left me with him and we soon started talking. Mr. Row had been practicing his profession in Port Sudan for some years and knew every rock in the harbor, where he dived, whenever he was needed, among the ships and along the quay wall.

"What is it you don't believe?" I asked him.

"The story of your swimming about among the reefs in bathing trunks. I know all about sharks. You can't put that one over on me."

We arranged that I would come and see him at the harbor one day. I had always meant to dive down, some time or other, to the submarine gardens in the entrance channel;

I was to show him, there, what I did and he was to look on.

The dance went on and on and on. Again I could hardly keep my eyes open. At last, about midnight, Bill had had enough and we drove back. Next morning Mahmud informed me that we couldn't go out that day; the wind was so high that we could never make the Wingate. Accordingly, I determined to spend the morning writing letters and afterward, about midday, to dive to the submarine gardens. Under the lee of the pier the water would still be smooth and clear, despite the wind.

Mr. Row fetched me in his car. When I showed him my mask, fins, and diving gear, he examined these articles with the air of an engineer who has been handed a toy locomotive. He himself dived in a submarine suit with a copper helmet and boots heavily weighted with lead. While we were driving round the harbor, he told me of the enormous blocks of dressed stone he was then salvaging from the rear section of the harbor. They came from the old quay wall, and I must be sure to photograph them. Stone blocks of that size had certainly never yet been photographed under water.

We passed the Customs barrier and drove as far as the last of the vessels lying at anchor alongside the quay. Here great bales of cotton were being loaded. Just clear of the ship's stern, near the tomb of the saint, from which several veiled ladies were watching me, I strapped on my equipment. While Mr. Row walked up and down on the quay and gave me some last-minute advice, I descended some steps and glided under water.

Apart from a layer of oil on the surface the water was

fairly clear. The quay wall went to a depth of some thirty feet and was encrusted with a great number of mussels and brightly colored plants. I was more interested, however, in the clearly visible hull of the ship, with its great screw, and a shoal of fat snappers hanging in a motionless cloud just behind the keel.

I had brought my harpoon. I swam cautiously back a little way toward the quay wall, then crossed over, beneath the vessel, and slipped alongside the keel in the direction of the screw. Here the water all round, as seen from the ship's shadow, resembled a pale-green curtain. The shoal of fish continued to hang motionless. Not until I was quite near did it begin to stir sluggishly. I harpooned in close proximity to the massive screw. There was a flurry of scales and the harpoon was nearly dragged out of my hand. Then its point came free in the water, and a fish with a big hole in its side made off into the distance.

Almost at the same moment, from the deep water where it was rather muddy and turbid, the big head of a jewfish bobbed up. He swam up a little way and stopped in clear water, standing out in gorgeous relief against the background of the pale-green curtain. Making up my mind in a flash, I returned to the surface, gave Mr. Row back the spear, which still held a shred of snapper skin, and took the camera in exchange. But of course, as soon as I got back, the jewfish had gone.

The submarine gardens beside the pier lay a little further off, toward the open sea. I swam along close to the pier at a depth of thirty feet. Looking up obliquely through the oily surface of the water, I could see the figures, somewhat distorted, of Mr. Row and two of the veiled women.

A few of the harbor employees had also come up and were staring down at me. All sorts of jetsam were lying about on the bottom, among the corals: there were ancient fragments of iron, crates, an automobile tire, and a lot of pots and pans.

The number of fish and other creatures in this area was amazing. In a cranny I found two crayfish, which were putting out immensely long, white feelers as they stalked about on their spidery legs. The lower depths, however, did not look by any means inviting. As sharks nearly always follow ships in the tropics, it was quite possible that one might pop up out of the turbid water. Accordingly, I stayed near the corals and kept a sharp lookout behind me and on both sides. I might have been swimming in this way for about twenty minutes, when I saw a big shadow above my head.

It was a boat. Certainly a very peculiar one, for it had a large, square window in the center of its substructure, through which several heads were peering down at the sea bed. It was the boat with the glass bottom! I hadn't noticed it while I was going down into the water near the ship. Apparently it had been repaired since I last heard of it and was once more in action. Consequently, I must now have reached those celebrated submarine gardens.

They were no different from the rest of the coral bottoms here in the harbor. There could be no comparison of them with the reefs outside. Meanwhile, the passengers on the boat had caught sight of me. I saw the heads dodging about excitedly, so I swam up and photographed them from below, through the plate-glass window, as they looked down.

I got quite a reception of "hello's" when I came to the surface. It turned out that the *"Ja-a-a, ja-a-a* lady" was among the tourists; she introduced me to the rest as I hung onto the side of the boat. One of the younger ladies asked me if I could fetch her a mussel; she ended by inviting me to have tea aboard her steamer. But as the ship in question was leaving shortly, I declined the invitation. Meantime, Mr. Row had vanished. Evidently he had gotten tired of waiting. When I told Bill that evening about the young lady, he explained to me that I had made an utter ass of myself.

"Why?" I asked.

"Would you like to know who she is?"

"Well?"

"I heard about her from the husband of the 'Ye-e-es, ye-e-es lady.' He was also on the boat and was very surprised at your refusing her invitation. Rumor on shipboard has it that the girl is the daughter of an owner of a big mine in South Africa. If you had only just made yourself a bit agreeable to her, the father might have financed an expedition for you, and maybe they would have come on it with you."

"I'd rather dive from a rowboat than take a woman on an expedition," I retorted. I was destined, as it happened, to change my views on that subject subsequently. When, three months later, I arrived for the second time in the Red Sea and explored the same reefs with several assistants, one of the pluckiest of my divers was—Lotte.

That evening it started raining. We had visitors and Bill once again astonished me by his social accomplishments. He had returned so late from the office that he had had no time to change. So he sat, quite at his ease, in shorts and a polo shirt, presiding at a table surrounded by black ties and low-cut dresses.

Two chairs remained unoccupied. Bill remembered, quite casually, that he had forgotten to ask the owner of the salt-works and his wife. The conversation turned, at first, to my meeting with the "dollar princess," then to the story of an old English archbishop who had turned over two pages during Divine Service, and finally to the subject of seamen and scuffles generally. Bill, to his great disgust, found he had no appetite and smoked a cigarette while we ate our filleted steaks.

"One day I was sitting in the bar at Shepheard's Hotel," he told us, "when a man at another table got up, came over to me, and said he didn't like the way I was looking at him. 'I'm most awfully sorry,' I answered, 'but I can assure you that until this moment I hadn't noticed you.'

" 'I suppose you think I have no business here?' was his next remark. 'Oh, no,' I replied, 'not at all.' And I asked him to have a whisky with me.

"And what do you think the fellow said to that? He was a seaman, you know. He stood quiet for a long time and thought it over. Then the said, 'No, I'd rather we went out-side. I don't want a drink. I want to give you a hiding.' "

With the object of making my own contribution to the entertainment of our guests, I told the story of the face Mahmud had made when I had offered him the ham roll.

"In Saudi Arabia," added Bill, "the import of ham to any part of the country is strictly forbidden. I have to send our ambassador there his ham in the official bag."

Everyone laughed.

The liqueur bottles went round, then the company drove, in several cars, to the movies. As I had already seen the film, I excused myself and went for an evening's stroll through the town. The rain had ceased, but the wind was blowing even harder. It carried the echoes of Arab-café music across the park into the dark streets. The signs hung out above the shops banged and clattered viciously against the walls. The streets were almost entirely empty. If I were unlucky, this sort of weather might go on for several days yet.

Next morning Mahmud reported that the sea was in a regular turmoil. The wind was whistling a monotonous serenade in the two palms that stood in front of the house. I spent the morning overhauling my gear and in the afternoon drove in Bill's car, armed with my camera, to the West African Village.

In contrast with the booths inhabited by the Fuzzy-Wuzzies, I found coconut groves here and streets bordered by high mud walls, with circular kraals behind them, topped by conical roofs of straw. Wherever the official car went, it aroused great attention. Men and women stood still in picturesque attitudes and looked steadily at me. I would lift up the camera, photograph them before they realized what was happening, and then we would drive on.

A young Negro woman ran after us and gave me to understand that she would be ready to let me photograph her unveiled. We posed her against a mud wall and I snapped the camera. She refused to accept any money. Either she wished to be immortalized, or else she was a leader of the local women's emancipation movement. Some of the men standing near gave her censorious glances. A little further on I saw a charming little female child in a lane.

I alighted cautiously and approached her, holding in my hand, by way of peace offering, like a stick of candy, a fivepiaster piece. The child took the coin without seeming to understand and stood motionless while I photographed her. Suddenly it seemed to dawn on her that she was to be the recipient of this enormous piece of luck, the possessor of all this wealth. A wide, blissful smile spread over her face; then an old woman dashed out of a doorway, there came the smack of a box on the ear, and the pitifully sobbing child was dragged into the house by the hair. Next moment the old woman appeared again, spat, and threw the coin at me. It is a superstition among these people that a photograph will rob them of a part of their personality. As I drove on, I thought sadly of my little friend, whom I had presented, in such quick succession, with unexpected good and ill fortune.

That evening a frightful storm broke out. It rained bucketsful and there were regular turns of lightning and thunder. Contrary to the usual social marathon, Bill and I had a quiet evening; we sat in the library and Bill read aloud to me the views of Bertrand Russell on Friedrich Nietzsche. In the afternoon a small parcel had arrived for me. It contained, in a matchbox, a live water beetle with yellow edges to the wings, and a brief note from one of the ladies of Port Sudan, asking me whether I could tell her what the creature was. She said she found it in the swimming pool.

The outdoors now became decidedly electric. "If it goes on like this," said Bill, "we shan't get any mail for two weeks. Our airfield can't stand much rain."

When I awoke next morning and went out on the balcony, I could hardly believe my eyes. The whole of the beautiful garden was under water! Of the lawn only a few islands still showed. Between the entrance steps and the garden gate one unbroken pond covered all the flower beds.

Bill stood with the gardener on a small peninsula. As soon as he saw me he called out plaintively, "What do you think of this? All the flowers we've just planted are ruined! And the beautiful lawn we spent so much money on is gone for certain!"

It rained, off and on, all the rest of the day; and all that night too; and the day after. One disaster after another was announced. The southern section of the road to Suakin became impassable; the water was a yard deep in that area and the violence of the current had carried away a taxi and capsized it. The airfield would be a swamp for weeks to come. In the West African Village several houses had been beaten down by the rain and washed away. Three people had been drowned, including the Red Sea Hotel cook. His body had been carried out to sea; it was found by mere chance, the head bitten off by a shark.

Bill was particularly worried about the golf course. "It'll cost us at least a hundred pounds to put that right again," he said.

I went down to the harbor on the second day and strolled out onto the pier. The sea presented an awe-inspiring spectacle. It was breaking over the lofty barriers of rock in gigantic waves and beyond them the sky over the curve of the reef was pitch-dark.

I could well imagine the tremendous excitement that was going on under water. A banquet would be in full swing, at which no one knew who would be served up next and who would be left over. Every second thousands of creatures would be dying in the the breakers; and tens of thousands would be fighting over the fragments, some to perish in the next few minutes. Natural selection would be working with more severity and implacability than ever. Any organism that was less than perfectly healthy and tough would go under in this merciless life-and-death struggle. And then, a few days later, the sea would be calm again, and in a trice the scene would be as gay and charming as before. Only the swollen bellies of the survivors would then indicate what had happened.

In the harbor whole tracts of seaweed were being driven along the surface, with transparent little jellyfish throbbing among them. Near the ships, for hundreds of yards round, lay shoals of sardines, so closely packed that from above they looked like a single compact mass. Just for fun, in spite of the turbidity of the water, I dived in among the fish. So long as I kept quiet they hemmed me in on every side and I felt the movement of a multitude of little bodies against my skin! If I moved, the living wall drew back as though at the wave of a magic wand.

Individuals did not exist in this mass of sardines; the entire shoal was one great superindividual, whose members seemed to obey one dominant will. Not a single fish left the ranks when the whole body wheeled. The subtle sensitivity of the creatures' lateral organs to oscillation kept them all linked to one another in a sort of electrical connection, and every impulse became a spark that exercised a common control over all their movements. If I remained still, individuals reappeared and the shoal advanced upon me with its hundreds of inquisitive eyes.

Finally, on the fourth day after the heavy rains, the sea had calmed down to such an extent that it was again possible to think of sailing. But Mahmud could not be found any-where. When, at last, Achmed produced him, he announced that the boat would have to be run ashore and cleaned up that day. I made a fuss and in an hour everything was ready. With a moderate wind at our backs we set off, over a ground swell that was still of considerable extent.

Though the water in the harbor remained a uniform yellow, beyond that area it turned, on the other side of a well-defined line, to a greenish-blue tint. I threw some stones which were lying in the boat into the water, to gauge from their visibility as they sank the extent to which the water had already clarified. We made for the *Umbrea* and tied up at the same mast as before. I had by this time obtained the diving permit.

Here, too, the water was still very turbid. When I went down to twenty-five or thirty feet, it grew a little clearer, and the milky haze was left behind, like a cloud, above my head. But even below this cloud cover I could only see at most thirty or thirty-five feet ahead. The storm had done all sorts of damage. The searchlight apparatus on deck aft had been broken. The harbor master had made me promise not to touch anything aboard in case it exploded. I couldn't help smiling at his caution—if I had had a thousand arms, I couldn't have knocked the vessel about as much as the storm had.

I didn't feel very comfortable aboard the *Umbrea* in that dark water, so I had the sail hoisted again, and we made for the end of the Wingate Reef, where I had dived the first afternoon. By this time I knew every nook and cranny of the place. Close to the coral rock the water was relatively clear, but I only had to swim out thirty feet in the direction

157

of the deep water to find myself at once in the midst of a milky shroud. It is possible that the clarity of water was caused by the corals themselves; the little polyps may have purified it with their tiny tentacles.

On this occasion I had the movie camera with me, and in the shallow water I took some close-ups of butterfly fish and corals. Suddenly, I heard excited shouts from the boat. Mahmud and O Sheik were standing up and pointing over my head to the sea in the distance. As the sunlight was also from that direction, I could see nothing but glittering, dazzling water out there.

"Girsch! Girsch!" they yelled excitedly. The word meant "sharks!"

So the great moment had arrived. As the water was roily, it was not much good to me. Involuntarily, my knees began to shake and I made off toward shallow water. Then I pulled myself together and swam quite calmly and coolly toward the boat, aboard which I clambered with some relief.

As I had been continually declaring that I only wished I could see some sharks, my present situation was rather delicate. If there really were any sharks about just now, I could hardly do less than dive and swim out to meet them, otherwise I should look a fool in front of the two natives. But to run such an unpredictable risk while the water was so thick would be sheer madness. For the second time during this expedition I found myself forced against my will to take a blind leap.

Both men were pointing to a certain spot, about a hundred yards from the place where I had been filming. As the sun was also in my eyes in that direction, it was some time before I saw anything. Odd, I thought, that two dorsal fins were to be seen there, racing about in apparently playful fashion. They looked remarkably soft and flexible and the interval between them remained the same all the time. Apparently, two sharks were playing about there, just below the surface.

The longer I watched them, the stranger the phenomenon seemed. First one fin would show up, then the other, then both together, while the distance between them always remained about fifteen feet.

"*Girsch kabir?*" I asked.

"*Kabir! Kabir!*" they both answered together. From their gestures it seemed that the sharks must be enormous. In addition, Mahmud tried to make me understand that some kind of a long, sharp point and some devil's horns were involved, but that could only be an expression of his luxuriant fancy. It was probable that both creatures were performing some sort of mating rite. The only queer thing was the soft and limp appearance of their dorsal fins.

"Up anchor!" I ordered. We might just as well row a little nearer, and then I could always decide, whether to enter the water or not. I tried to subdue my mounting excitement, but I couldn't manage it. Somehow it seemed to me that until this moment I had very happily been skating over thin ice, which now suddenly developed widening cracks.

The anchor was stuck in the corals; despite strenuous tugging by both men, it would not come loose. I swung myself overboard and dived down. I was surprised to find myself repeatedly puffing against the deep water. I really should have to keep my nerves steady! I cleared the anchor in a hurry and swam up again to the boat.

I gave orders to row with great caution, avoiding splashes.

The two fins had retreated some distance, but still remained clearly visible. As we drew slowly nearer to them, I hastily put a new film into the still-photograph camera. Then, suddenly, the two fins disappeared.

I didn't know whether to be disappointed or relieved. My curiosity as to what sort of sharks these were and what they were up to had become intense. All the same, I told myself, in present circumstances this was the best thing that could have happened.

Then the fins showed up again!

Mahmud and O Sheik looked at me expectantly. Well, so be it! I had already slipped on my fins and buckled on my knife. I hurriedly adjusted the sling of the camera round my neck, drew the mask over my eyes, and slid into the water.

All round me the water was green and turbid. I could estimate to some extent, from the dark hull of our boat, the distance I could see through the gloom. It would be from twenty to twenty-five feet at most. At all events, if I got near enough, I might perhaps, even in this fog, take some exceptional photographs. On condition, to be sure, that I still retained all my limbs undamaged!

As I swam in the direction of the soft, bobbing fin tips we had so clearly seen above the waves, I stared ahead with such intensity that my eyes smarted. Now that I had made up my mind to swim there, anxiety and fear were forgotten. All I wanted now was to catch sight of them. Everything else would then follow automatically.

Suddenly, the fins disappeared.

I was sure I was in the immediate neighborhood of the creatures; I knew that instinctively, but I had no idea where they were. As I glided to and fro in the yellowish-green fog, I glanced up at the boat. Mahmud and O Sheik were on their feet, gazing at the water. Obviously, they, too, couldn't see anything. To avoid being surprised, I turned in a circle and looked all around me. All the time I kept gasping, though only spasmodically, for air. It was a distressing situation. The strain of staring had brought tears to my eyes. Then I became conscious that something big was coming up on my left.

I had a physical intuition of the thing before I actually saw it. Then I perceived a dim outline, which resembled an enormous blanket rather than a living sea-being. I concentrated my whole attention upon the slowly approaching monster. In the center of its gigantic body yawned a quadrangular mouth of tremendous size. A light broke in upon me at last! The two fins I had seen, that always kept fifteen feet apart, did not belong to two sharks but to a single monstrous beast that seemed quite endless in this opaque water.

At that very critical moment I absolutely had to have some air. I rose above the surface, then immediately dived again and stared ahead. The sight that I now confronted appeared almost incredible, even to myself. The huge beast had come still nearer, had turned round a little, and now I had a profile view; I could see one eye and above it—two projecting devil's horns!

I only caught a glimpse of them for the fraction of a second. Then the water in front of me swept into violent foaming movement. A broad, whirling flipper brushed me aside; I was caught among eddies and spun round in a surge of bubbles. A thin, black object shot past me—and the vision vanished.

Only the slowly ascending stream of air bubbles proved that it had not been all my imagination. Back in the boat, it took quite a time before I recovered from my excitement. I was not to discover for another week what it really was that I had seen.

THE FIRST SHARKS

THE FIRST SHARKS

I HEARD the usual clatter close to my head. Achmed was again placing the teapot, cup, and the little saucer with the three sweet biscuits on the table by my bed. Then he drew the curtains back. It was a Sunday, the third since my arrival. We were to make a special day of it. Bill intended to take me to a reef a long way off, where sharks were said to be especially numerous.

Bill, still half asleep, poked his head into the room. "That cursed whisky!" he exclaimed.

"Those cursed invitations!" I retorted, with similar fervor. Though we had only had four hours' sleep, we were soon ready, and shortly afterward down at the harbor. Mahmud had stepped a mast twice as high as usual in the boat; it was like a great sloping tree and carried a sail of vast dimensions. As our narrow boat only had a very small wooden keel, it was something of a puzzle why we didn't capsize under such a spread of canvas.

In honor of the distinguished passenger the boat had

been scrupulously cleaned up and the daintiest of mats laid out. In addition, Bill had brought a number of cushions with him, on which we made ourselves comfortable amidships. It was still rather early and the harbor looked quite dead and deserted. There wasn't a breath of air, but as soon as the sail had been set, we were off.

The efficiency of that sail was a miracle. It seemed able to catch the gentlest puff of air from heaven, and fast and silently, as though in play, we glided on our way.

While Bill smoked his inevitable cigarettes, I lay on my back and watched the masthead rocking to and fro against the clear morning sky. I tried to imagine the entire vast expanse of sea, with all its submarine towers and bastions, and myself gliding high above them, a tiny little creature at the ultimate peak of that immeasurable space.

I envisioned the armies of fishes charging about there; the shoals of jellyfish and cephalopods and the gaily colored swarm in each drop of water. Even if I could get down to depths of five or ten hundred feet, I should still only be standing on the outermost, topmost verge of that unimaginably profound abyss. The average depth of the oceans amounts to no less than thirteen thousand feet! How many living beings, never yet seen by human eye, must be hidden in those endless spaces!

I tried to imagine the first beasts creeping ashore out of the sea and gradually developing into the entire collection of land animals, including man himself. Man now controlled dry land, and all its other inhabitants submitted to his will. He allowed them to live, bred them if he chose, or caged and exterminated them if he so desired. But his will had not yet made itself known in the sea. Shyly and yet confidingly the fishes which had never seen a man before would come to look at me. What presentiments might be theirs! Of some strange revolution of time, perhaps, when after millions of years human life was returning to its original source and home?

Port Sudan now lay far behind us. We were following the coast in a northerly direction, but on a slanting course away from it. The mountain ranges could now hardly be distinguished among the distant banks of clouds. Here and there the first faint breaths of wind ruffled the calm water. It looked as though the wind were trying to tickle the sea out of its inertia.

Bill was gossiping with Mahmud, who was steering.

"What does he say?" I inquired, as a short silence fell.

"He's giving me the local news," Bill answered. "The railway was functioning again yesterday, for the first time, and the train ran over a Fuzzy. I feel sorry for those fellows, but one can't break them of the habit. When they feel tired they use the rails as pillows."

"Use the rails as pillows? The actual lines themselves?"

"Yes. In the desert they've got nothing that does so well for leaning one's head against. And unfortunately they sleep like logs. Mahmud was also telling me that the boat must definitely be run ashore and cleaned up. He says he knows perfectly well that the boat's done for and he and his family will have to starve, but for the good of the Sudan and in particular for the sake of His Excellency, our guest, et cetera, et cetera."

"But the boat's not his property at all!"

"Of course it isn't. He's just a rascal, that's all."

On the horizon, far out to sea, an indistinct shape, resembling a reduced silhouette of the Eiffel Tower, could be seen. Bill told me it was the lighthouse on Sanganeb, an atoll situated on the outermost fringe of the coral reefs. If I were interested, he said, I could visit it on a Thursday aboard the supply vessel. He added that the lighthouse staff were Egyptians who were relieved only every four months and thus were delighted when anyone came to see them.

"If you ever do return here sometime with a fairly large party, that would be quite a good place for you to camp out. There's any amount of room in the lighthouse and the atoll is extremely interesting. Plenty of hammerhead sharks about, too."

I requested Bill to ask Mahmud whether we could expect to find true sharks anywhere near the reef we were then making for.

"I don't have to ask him that," Bill retorted. "There are huge sharks there, I know that myself. Last time we went to the place, when I caught a bayard, we had no less than six round the boat, for I counted them."

"How big were they?"

"Between five and ten feet long. There was one that may have been even bigger."

"Were they gray sharks?"

"I didn't look closely enough at them to tell. But I think they were. At any rate, one had a ghastly great mouth on him and was so bold that we had to use the oar to keep him from coming aboard."

The wind had freshened and we were making better and better time. Under Mahmud's directions O Sheik fixed a plank to the boat's hull in such a way that it stuck out a good five feet from the side, outrigger style. Then he crawled out onto it, thus providing a counterpoise to the sail.

"Look! Over there!"

Bill jumped up. I just had time to catch sight of a big tail before it vanished into the sea. A moment or two later the fish leaped for the second time. It was a sailfish! Including the sword projecting from the head it must have measured well over six feet. The notched sail towering from its back quivered and glittered gloriously in the sunlight. For a second the fish glided through the air, hardly sixty feet from the boat, flashing like molten metal. Then he dived, sword foremost, back into the water, leaving nothing but a ring of foam to show where he had gone.

Bill hurriedly extracted from the leaden box which held all his hooks his biggest spoon spinner and made it fast to his line. Shortly after he had made his cast, the reel sang out; and after a short but strenuous tussle we landed a fine Caranx.

The dexterity with which Mahmud steered us between the reefs, which now became steadily more numerous, was amazing. Some could be identified by their crests of foam, but there were also a great many which were completely invisible in the glittering water. On one occasion he took us, at a giddy speed, through a narrow channel that couldn't have been more than thirty feet wide.

The sun was already quite high when we finally reached our destination, after two-and-a-half hours' sailing. We anchored in deep water at a little distance from a long wall of reef. Bill had ordered O Sheik to cut a slice from the Caranx; this he fastened to a handline, which he let down into the deep water.

"You can catch mice with bacon," he said, "but if it's shark we want, we can't do better than one of the big groupers that are so numerous about here—Ow! Quick, quick! Get him! Get him!"

The line, with a terrific jerk, had suddenly started to run out. Bill tried to hang onto it, but the pull was too much for him and took off a bit of his skin. Mahmud and O Sheik, almost simultaneously, grabbed the line, which instantly dragged them both overboard, head first. Mahmud managed to get a grip on the boat's side with one hand, while with the other he held onto the line like grim death. Either the fish would pull the boat under as well as the line or else Mahmud's desperate effort would bring him to a halt.

We rocked as though in a storm. But the fish had, in fact, been stopped. After the failure of his first dash for freedom his subsequent struggles were only half as wild. While Bill and I made the line fast, the other two clambered back into the boat as fast as they could. Then Mahmud saw that he had lost his turban in the fracas and jumped into the water again. We still hadn't seen any sharks. After we had recovered from the shock to some extent and were hauling in the fish, we all laughed heartily.

Bill's laughter, however, was mingled with groans over his torn palm. By slow degrees we managed to get the fish alongside and Mahmud hooked him aboard with the gaff. It was a magnificent grouper, spotted red and blue and weighing a good forty or fifty pounds. Mahmud had only just stopped him in time, for if he had reached his lair in the rock, we should probably never have gotten him out.

We then anchored the boat closer to the edge of the reef, and I began to explore the submarine world, diving without my respirator. Bill watched with a sour smile. He was obviously envying me my swim.

"Come along in!" I called to him. "You'll be perfectly all right. Take my spare mask and come along in!"

"I'm not quite mad yet!" he shouted back. But next moment it looked as though he had changed his mind. I saw him trying on the mask; but immediately afterward he pushed it back up on his forehead.

"It suffocates you! How do you manage to breathe with the thing?"

"Breathe with your mouth. And spit on the glass first, then wipe it and rinse it again. Otherwise it gets misted under water."

Bill duly spat, shaking his head, then did a handspring overboard. The first glance he took under water made him forget all the sharks and other monsters in the sea world. He made Mahmud give him my spare fins and was soon swimming in the shallows over the reef.

"Ow! Ow! Ow!" I suddenly heard him shout. "Get away, get away, you brute!"

I hastened to his assistance. There was a grazed spot on Bill's calf and it was being nibbled by a small, worm-shaped fish. The creature was creeping slyly over the skin and waiting for the leg to stop moving. When it did, he bit the sore place with ferocious energy. Between us, we put the little wretch to flight.

"Did you ever see little fish being caught by those big sea anemones?" Bill asked me.

The entire side of a single rock was occupied by one of the giant anemones he referred to. Among its many hundreds of tentacles, fatal to all fishes, tiny pomacentrids were playing about, thoroughly at home there. The specially puzzling question in regard to this queer association was how the anemone recognized these little fish as its friends while swallowing all the rest. Mutual affection went so far that the fishlets, when alarmed, actually took refuge in the anemone's maw, the very place where all other fish were digested.

"They clean her up," I explained to Bill. "They devour all her parasites and so, of course, in return for services rendered they are allowed to hide in her."

Bill didn't look as if he intended ever to come out of the water. He found a sea urchin with red, claviform prickles between two rocks and tried to pull it out. He puffed, snorted, emerged, dived down again.

As the camera had gotten stuck again, I decided to take my spear and respirator and go hunting. The place seemed very promising. There were considerably more fishes about here than at the Wingate Reef, and coral formations, such as I had never seen, were dimly visible in the depths.

I glided down without further ado. I found myself in what appeared to be an oriental city full of temples, that had sunk beneath the waves, its ruins overgrown with creeping plants of a hundred hues. Castles of coral, thirty and thirty-five feet high, towered up, their battlements gorgeously adorned with numbers of small turrets. Among them precipitous defiles wound like streets through the rock. The amazing color of this vision was due to the extraordinarily rich growth of leather corals, spreading everywhere like a primitive forest of luxuriant vegetation. Unlike the rock corals, these had not developed from a chalk foundation, and their polyps had not six, but eight tentacles, which were, moreover, feathered. They opened out like thousands and thousands of little stars, pulsated rhythmically, and drew in their tiny heads as I approached.

Brownish-yellow catkins grew everywhere, resembling clumps of pulpy bracken. The delicately blooming sprigs of prickly Alcyonaria branched out in every direction, glimmering with lilac or reddish hues. Grayish-blue Xenia corals grew out of beds of orange-tinted and deep-black dermoid Alcyonaria, with delicate polyps bearing diminutive violet and reddish-purple stars.

Among the many fishes that fluttered like insects and birds among the ruins of this sunken city two big dark groupers took a special interest in my arrival. They pursed their thick, puffy lips inquisitively in my direction and stared gloomily at me with their goggle eyes. But in spite of these signs of friendly attention they kept well out of the way of my harpoon, though resplendent yellow angelfish came dancing right up to me and took their time to look me over.

The streets of the coral city led obliquely downward and ended in a precipice falling almost vertically into the depths. When I reached this point in the jungle of coral, twenty or thirty blue-black fish ascended from the depths. Their shape and the double quill of their tails indicated a close relationship to the green rhinoceros fish, though their heads were hornless. I gave them the name of "boobyfish," for they were really exceptionally silly. They swam, with frank curiosity, right up to the gleaming point of the harpoon, examined it with the greatest assurance, turned this way and that around it, and brought their little snouts close to the sharp tip as if they meant to use it as a flute.

I soon made up my mind and ran the point of the harpoon through the body of the first one. The point came free, the fish wriggled frantically on the harpoon, and I was dragged behind the shaft through the corals. The strength of the creature was amazing. After it had described, at lightning speed, a number of figures of eight, the wire that attached the point to the short length of cord on the shaft of the harpoon broke. The fish vanished in a side alley.

The other members of the shoal surrounded me in the greatest excitement. If I had still had a point on my harpoon, I should have been able to send it through any of them I chose. But that excellent point of mine was gone now, unfortunately. I had to come to the surface and fetch another.

The entire sea bed had risen in revolt. Small fishes, as though attracted by a magnet, had fled to the shelter of the gaily colored vegetation of the rocks; but they now reappeared and spread out till all the rocks seemed to increase in size. No fewer than three large and four small spiny-rayed perch had risen from the depths and were staring inquisitively up at me as they flapped their fins. A moray eel stuck its ugly head out of a hole. An enormous, angular fish came spiraling diagonally upward toward me with irresolute movements. I kept a sharp lookout in all directions, in case a shark, too, might turn up. But except for a few mackerel that arrived full tilt, in the guise of camp followers, and also made me the center of a merry-go-round, the fishy tumult had now subsided again.

Bill was quite surprised to see me return to the boat so quickly.

"Anything wrong?" he called.

"Oh, no. Quite the contrary!" I cried back breathlessly. I waved the broken wire at him and told him what had happened.

As the wire attached to the other points was also by this

time a bit old and rather rusty, I swung myself into the boat and tied on some new wire. In addition, I fastened a double line to the shaft this time, by way of reinforcement. Those blue fish were not going to get away from me again if I could help it.

They were, in fact, on the spot once more when I descended. But their attitude was now distinctly less enterprising. The change may have been partly due to the "panic-creating material" which, when a fish is injured, is distributed through the water from its skin, gradually spreads, and warns other members of the species that danger threatens in the neighborhood.

I decided to swim a bit deeper into the abyss, till I reached undisturbed regions again. The growth of coral was just as fantastic down there. Several fish past which I swam watched me from their holes as though I were a sea monster on the prowl. And I really felt rather like one as I swam along, filled with the lust of the chase, looking for new adventures, with my harpoon ready. I stopped beneath a high, jagged cliff. From this vantage ground I had a clear view of the corals to right and left and of the abyss. I could not foresee at the time that this rock was destined to come within an ace of representing my tombstone.

At the rear of the cavity, which formed a kind of recess, I saw a fine golden perch, lying motionless and calmly looking at me. As it couldn't get away, I could have easily harpooned it. But I didn't in the least want to do so. I was only interested in those silly "boobyfish" which had been so impudently wheeling round and round the harpoon.

I didn't have to wait long for a chance at them. Here, too, I had already been spotted by one of their shoals and it came dancing right up to me. I aimed at the fattest and harpooned it. As before, the fish dashed frantically off, but this time the wire and line held, and I myself was straddling the corals in such a way that the creature could tug and wriggle as much as it liked but couldn't get free. It drifted in space like a flag, at the end of the taut line.

A torrent of fish poured over us while I was doing my best to haul in the catch and get hold of it. At last I had the creature by the tail and finished it off with my knife. A cloud of blood spread out above us. Then a black shadow came gliding diagonally down, from one side.

I was so busily engaged in working the point loose, as it had gotten stuck in the fish, that I didn't see the shadow until it was within a couple of yards of me. When I looked up, I saw a phalanx of threatening pairs of eyes directed upon me. No less than forty barracudas, each five feet long, were coming straight at me in a silent wedge.

I had met these dreaded killers of the seas before, in the West Indies. We had come across even bigger specimens there, but always solitary rovers, which had not attacked us. I had never seen such a shoal as this before; perhaps Bill, Mahmud, and all the rest of them had not been so mistaken, after all, to warn me as seriously against barracudas as against sharks.

It is true that barracudas do not, like sharks, bite off whole limbs at once; nevertheless, their habit is to rush upon their victim from all directions and tear his flesh from his bones into strips, the taste of blood exciting them to a state of utter frenzy. A lady I knew was only about thirty feet away from a man when the latter was attacked, at Bali, in water only up to his hips, by barracudas. Though

I looked up and saw a phalanx of threatening eyes directed upon me. No less than forty barracudas were coming straight for me.

Camera failure was a constant bogy. Here I am doing some minor repair in the boat.

I saw a great gray shape come gliding through the circle of barracudas. A shark! It was about eight feet long and had white tips to its back and tail fins.

Each time I surfaced after invading the wonders of the coral reefs, it seemed as though I had returned from another world.

I stopped beneath a high, jutting cliff of coral. With its protective wall at my back, I lay in wait for Red Sea sharks.

From the boat Bill watched me through the waterscope as I glided down into the depths in search of fish. Clad in my diving equipment, I held the spear in my right hand, with two lines dangling from it— one connected the shaft of the harpoon to my shoulder, the other was to be attached to the coral stump.

several persons at once rushed to his assistance, and got him ashore, he was so badly wounded that a leg had to be amputated and in the end he succumbed.

The innumerable teeth in the jaws of a barracuda resemble little daggers. I regarded the creatures with a certain uneasiness as they, with their staring, expressionless eyes, made steadily toward me.

I got a firm hold on the shaft of my harpoon—the point was still stuck in the "boobyfish," which lay on the corals at my feet—and backed away into the recess. I was at bay now, like a rat in its hole.

The barracudas patrolled the entrance tirelessly, back and forth, coming a little nearer to me each time they turned. It was a regular siege. But they had not yet made up their minds to give the signal for the assault. Just as when I had been surrounded by the shoal in the harbor, I now, too, had the feeling that I was not confronted by individual creatures but by a sort of superego, with a steadily mounting common will. I could see no escape and began to lose my composure. I started jabbing viciously, in all directions, at one fish after another, with the blunt end of the iron shaft.

I damaged a few of them, but the reaction to this move was to increase the weird horror of the scene. The fish described a circle at lightning speed and were back again in their original order the next moment, just as though they were all enclosing an electrical field, each member keeping relentlessly to its appointed position.

In this situation an unexpected ally came to my rescue. I saw a great gray shape come gliding through the circle of barracudas, followed closely by a second. Sharks! They were about eight feet long, well proportioned, and had white tips to their back and tail fins. The sight of them caused the barracudas to cower like dwarfs. For a moment I plucked up courage; I dashed suddenly in among the barracudas, simultaneously making as much noise as I could by puffing against the water. The shoal scattered in all directions, and my repeated antics prevented it from reassembling. The common will that so mysteriously and invisibly dominated them went to pieces.

Sharks! There they were at last! A third was just approaching from the left, zooming up, like an aircraft, between two towers of coral. He glided nearer, across a ravine of coral, and swam past me, a bare six feet above my head. Then he turned, so as to focus me with his laterally placed eyes. It was the first time I had seen a shark vertically, from below: his belly, with the pectoral fins standing out from it like pointed wings, was snow-white; at its forward end, behind the tapering snout, showed a clear, semilunar outline—the jaws.

I felt marvelously self-confident again. No, these sharks, I perceived immediately, were no different from those I already knew. They were, so to speak, old friends, whose actions and behavior I could rely on without question. At last the suspense under which I had so long labored was at an end—the fabulous bogies, capable of every atrocity, had turned into ordinary creatures of flesh and blood with which I was perfectly familiar from hundreds of previous encounters. For the first time I no longer felt myself to be a surreptitious invader of these reefs, but their ruler. Like a protective, invulnerable coat of mail, a feeling of power and security enveloped me.

The first three sharks had now disappeared and a smaller one, darkly colored, had risen from the abyss. I swam toward him and he turned sluggishly away. The battle was over! The barracudas hung in a motionless cloud a hundred feet away. Perhaps that malign instrument was again playing upon a uniform will, that common electrical vibration directed to the annihilation of a new victim. I swam to the edge of the abyss and looked down into the black, unknown depths, where I could see the shapes of more sharks. Then the risen tide of my confidence ebbed again, and I decided to call it a day. I went back to the rock under which the golden perch was still hovering and fetched my dead "booby-fish," which probably weighed a good fifteen or twenty pounds. Then I glided up the coral precipice, with considerable relief.

I couldn't stop myself from continuously chuckling into the respirator. It may have been the reaction from my excitement. On the way up I came unexpectedly upon our boat's anchor, with part of its severed cable still attached. I dragged it up to the top of the reef and looked across the water, finding that the boat had drifted quite a distance away. I shouted, and Mahmud rowed over. Between us we knotted the strands together again.

Bill looked at me in rather a disconcerted fashion when I told him, laughing, about the sharks and barracudas. "You don't mean to tell me seriously that there were sharks in the vicinity while I was swimming about in the water?"

"Yes, of course I do," I chuckled. "And a pack of barracudas in the bargain!"

It was not until I was in the boat, telling the story, that I really regained my self-possession. Mahmud, when Bill interpreted my tale to him, rolled his eyes and shook his head. He passed on the story to O Sheik, who only understood Fuzzy-Wuzzy talk and probably, after interpolation, gathered that the sharks had been twice their actual size. When I had finished speaking, Mahmud solemnly walked over to me, laid his hand on my shoulder, and informed me that my name would in future be "Big Shark." I was always afterward known by this name among the natives.

That evening, as Bill and I were sitting at our ease over our whisky, he told me he had had similar experiences with crocodiles.

"In the Dinka District, where I was Commissioner for two years, there are any amount of them in the rivers," he said. "Once, when I was fishing, my spinner caught on something and my boy jumped overboard and dived down to free it. But he couldn't loosen it right away and told me when he got back that there were two crocodiles lying down there.

" 'Well,' I said to him, 'then for God's sake get back into the boat. We'll write off that spoon, in fact we might just as well cut the line!' But no, he said, it would be a pity to lose that lovely spinner; and he went and fetched it. During the next hour I saw four big crocodiles swim past at that very spot.

"But the boys would never enter waters where a hippo was known to be. I said to one of them, 'You don't worry about crocs, why should you bother about hippos?' But they refused point-blank to chance it! You see, the crocodile is sacred to them, and they are quite convinced that it will do them no harm. I suppose that, as they don't feel fear, they get away with it. The brutes must understand that, somehow or other."

At night I couldn't get to sleep for a long time. I kept thinking of the Red Sea sharks I had met that day. I compared them with those I had known previously and tried to recall every detail of their behavior and movements. I drew up, mentally, a plan of action which would enable me to photograph them.

I would go to the same spot, sit down on some convenient coral, and fasten a fairly long rope to the tip of my harpoon, not connected with the shaft, but tied to the coral beside me. Then I would harpoon another "boobyfish." It would be held close to the coral by the rope, would not distract me by its struggles, and would attract sharks and barracudas to the spot, while I held the camera ready to photograph them.

I would fasten the harpoon shaft to my shoulder, as I had formerly fastened the yardstick, so that I could get at it instantly if I wanted to. I would also take a reserve barb and roll of line with me in my breastpocket. If one "boobyfish" were not enough, I would quickly tie the second line to the rock and fix the second barb in one of the fish that would be surrounding me.

In the morning I started, first thing, on the repair of my camera. Obviously the salad oil I had used for lubricating had not been right for the job. I soon found that this time there was no avoiding it. I must take the mechanism to pieces down to the last tiny wheel. When I came to a certain screw I stopped. There was one part that I could loosen either from above or from below, but if I didn't do it properly two little springs, which I could clearly see, would fly out; and it was quite possible that after that I would never be able to reassemble the mechanism.

Bill advised me to apply to a certain watchmaker in the town, who had the reputation of being a genius. I lost no time and found the gentlemen, a fat Indian, surrounded by a group of earnest admirers, to whom he was just then explaining some point in the works of an opened watch.

He seemed a little vexed at my interruption and requested me to return in ten days' time, as he was overwhelmed with orders at present. But as soon as I mentioned the name of the Commissioner, he became more accessible. He screwed his pocket lens into his eye and turned the mechanism this way and that under it. I explained the situation to him and described my problem about the two little springs. Thereupon he took from the drawer of his bench, which was crammed with watch components, a small screw driver and began to apply it, with some impetuosity, to bending the wheelwork first in one direction and then in another.

"Do please be careful!" I said. "You simply can't—" I didn't get any further. The fellow had opened up the whole thing with one vigorous jerk and the two little springs came flying out!

"Keep still, every one of you!" I yelled at the startled group of spectators.

While they all stood as if turned to stone, I started crawling about on the floor among the natives' dirty bare feet, searching for springs which were barely visible to the naked eye. By a miracle I found them, each one near a big toe. After that I made the man of genius supply me with a little watchmaker's oil and then left his premises, quivering with rage.

As soon as I got home I tried to make out what the little springs were for. The smallest, as I now saw for the first time, was broken. After several hours' work I managed to replace it with another. By midnight the shutter was functioning for the first time.

Next day I took some experimental pictures of an improvised pendulum, in order to find out whether the shutter speeds had altered, and if so to what extent. Achmed had to hold a heavy weight suspended and let it swing, at the word of command, close in front of me and my poised camera. From the degree of blurring I calculated the amount of variation. The hundredth part of a second had become an eightieth and the two hundredth a hundred and thirtieth. I was more concerned at the fact that the slide still only gave a demi-exposure. I again had to take the whole camera to pieces. Not until evening did I get it to work properly again.

On the following day, at eleven o'clock in the morning, we were once more lying at anchor where I had seen the sharks. Bill, who happened to be free that day, had again accompanied me. This time we were equipped with a waterscope (a submarine telescope—a watertight square box, or tube, with a sheet of glass at its lower end) through which he could watch me from the deck of the boat. If I sat on the top of one of the coral castles, he could still see from up above.

Hung round with various objects, like a Christmas tree, I glided down into the depths. The submarine camera was slung across my chest, together with the submarine light gauge; and in my right hand I held the spear, with two lines hanging from it, a long one for fastening to the coral and a short one by which the shaft of the harpoon was tied to my shoulder. After a brief search I found a stump of coral shaped like an armchair. I first made sure, by groping round it, that it was not upholstered with stinging moss animals; then I sat down in it.

In accordance with my preconceived plan of campaign I tied the line to a ledge. The light gauge gave me the correct exposure; I calculated the range at two meters—I hoped the sharks would come as near as that. I also hoped, but hardly dared to expect, that one of the sharks would snap up the harpooned fish that would be struggling in open water. If I succeeded in photographing such an incident at the right moment, I should have made a long stride forward toward my cherished ambition of a research vessel. Such a picture would not only be published all over the world and bring in money but would also assuredly impress the film distributor upon whose good box offices my next project would depend.

A shoal of "boobyfish" duly approached. I chose the fattest; but I was a bit too sure of myself, harpooned too soon, and fell short of the mark. The fish all made off in a panic. Then they returned and formed a circle round me, about five or ten feet away. But they wouldn't come any nearer. As I had company, for each of my movements was being watched from above through the glass screen, I was doubly mortified by my lack of success.

In order to attract again the attention of the inquisitive fish upon myself, I rose from my seat and began to go through all sorts of acrobatic contortions. Mahmud and O Sheik, as Bill told me later, went into absolute ecstasies over this performance. The "boobyfish" were also obviously delighted with my efforts to entertain them. All the same, they wouldn't come any nearer.

My annoyance and exertions increased my rate of breathing. Those fish were really too stupid for words! Instead of coming the least bit closer, they hovered irresolutely about and stuck their little snouts out toward me. I tried to approach them with the harpoon by swimming, but they retreated before me as fast as I advanced. I was, moreover, attached to the coral stump by the line and so had only a limited range of action. Everything I had planned had gone hopelessly wrong!

I had to start puffing in order to regain my balance. Then both patience and impatience had their reward, but from a different direction. Two big bayards appeared in the distance, playing some sort of game with each other. They swam straight toward me and, though the biggest weighed at least forty pounds, I did not hesitate to pink him neatly through the body.

He dashed wildly away and the usual fishy-go-round dance began. I was still so furious with the "boobyfish" that I rapidly fastened the second line to my belt, stuck the barb on the end of it, and ran the nearest of the creatures through. In the twinkling of an eye the "boobyfish" had pulled me off the stump; I caught my left fin in the other line, at the end of which the big bayard was struggling. As a result I was thrown on my back, close to the trunk of coral, in open water, while two powerful fish tugged me in opposite directions. Water had gotten into my mask and the light

185

gauge was squeezing my respirator flat. If I were now charged by sharks or barracudas, they could take any bites at me they liked.

In company with the struggling fish I dropped down twenty-five feet, as far as the base of the coral stump. Because I was hopelessly entangled in two separate ropes and was meanwhile desperately trying to force my knife out of its rubber sheath, in which it had slipped a bit too far, I had no chance to manipulate the breathing valve. Owing to the sudden descent and consequent alteration of pressure, my respirater was now completely flat.

I felt that I was suffocating. A sense of utter emptiness rose from my stomach into my chest, and I began to pant convulsively. Then at last I got the knife out and cut away one of my bonds. As my mask had filled with water, I was almost blind. I thought I caught sight of a shark, struck out madly in all directions, and kept pressing on the valve until I suddenly realized that there was no more oxygen— the cylinder was empty. This meant that I was now several pounds too heavy and would have to fight my way back to the surface by sheer force.

I gave the rock a hard kick and felt the trapped fin work loose from the second rope. The submarine camera had slipped round to my back and was strangling me. There was only one thing for it now—to the surface! I had become so overheated that I was trembling all over. Then, after what seemed an eternity, I noticed that the water was growing clearer. I broke the surface, tore the respirator hose from my mouth and the mask from my eyes, sank again, after so deep an intake of air that it nearly deprived me of my senses, rose once more, and used up the last of my strength in a final dash to the edge of the reef. I clung to it, utterly exhausted, till the boat rowed across and picked me up.

"That was really marvelous," was the first remark I heard from Bill. "I never saw anything like it in my life before!"

His bird's-eye view must have made the whole thing look like a glorious battle. He told me, breathlessly, that two sharks had come up quite close to me and "looked on," just as he had.

Lying flat on my back in the boat, I came to my senses only very gradually. I had swallowed a lot of water as I broke the surface and was feeling deadly sick. My heart was thumping as if it were going to split. Whenever I closed my eyes I could see innumerable fish circling round, above, and below me.

It was not until after we had had lunch in the boat that I felt fit enough to re-enter the water. The two lines with the fish attached to them were still down there among the corals. Mahmud affirmed that he had seen through the waterscope that the lines I had cut had again gotten tangled in the corals. Both had been partly drawn under the rocks; nothing was to be seen of the fish attached to them.

The spot was only about fifty or sixty feet down, and I chose to dive into the sea without equipment. At a depth of thirty-five feet I stopped exhaling and swallowed; by that activity the pressure was relaxed and I went down a bit further. With sound ears and the eustachian tubes free from catarrh, you can get down, with two such pauses, to sixty or seventy-five feet.

I first cut the line free that was fastened to the rock and had the bayard hanging at the end of it. I succeeded, on the second attempt, in dragging the fish out of the hole at the base of the coral stump. Only the short end of him was left. The rest had been enjoyed by a moray eel or some other fish.

While I was trying to detach the "boobyfish" as well—it had swum through several holes in the rock before the line had got caught up again—I perceived that there were barracudas hanging motionless in the deep water a little way off. I dashed off to fetch the camera and swam down to them, without equipment. I stopped some distance away and remained quite still. Then they turned and approached me. I managed to get some good photographs. I returned to the boat, put in a color film, and repeated all my shots in color.

After this I felt I had had enough.

As darkness began to close in we came once more to Port Sudan. At home I found a large official envelope lying on my bed. It contained a very formal invitation from His Excellency, the British Governor-General, to the reception in Khartoum. The reception was due to take place in six days' time.

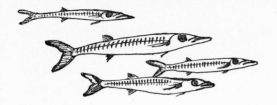

THE KING'S BIRTHDAY

THE KING'S BIRTHDAY

I SPENT THE DAY before our departure for Khartoum in diving strenuously. I felt, while thus engaged, that the interruption had come just at the right time. I had cuts and scratches all over my body, and they would only heal if I kept out of salt water for a few days. On my left arm, where a big starfish had stung me, some rather disagreeable symptoms of paralysis had begun to appear. I could no longer raise the affected arm higher than my shoulder.

I saw sharks every day now and had several good opportunities to photograph them. It really seemed as if they had been off on a trip somewhere and were now back home again. It was especially toward evening, when the light under water assumed a peculiar chalky tint, that I hardly ever failed to encounter them. There were times when I turned round suddenly and found a shark just behind me. But the sight of the beasts, even when their unexpected appearance startled me, always gave me pleasure.

No other sea creature can compare with a shark in beauty

of form and grace of movement. Porpoises, under water, look fidgety and awkward; tunnies resemble robots, rushing along in their senseless sort of way as if they had just been wound up; rays always give the impression of grotesque deformity. But the shark is at one with his watery environment. It seems to help him along, so to speak, in the splendid perfection of his sweeping glide, and he looks as much at home there as a cat among down pillows in a bed.

My fearlessness protected me better than dagger and spear. The sharks evidently respected me as of equal rank with themselves, and nothing in my behavior called for an attack. You can have any illusions you please about the kings among animals, but there is one thing they are not: brave fighters. Cautiously, warily, and ready to run, they hunt creatures weaker than themselves. Only at mating time, when driven by their instincts, do they sometimes attack opponents equal or superior to themselves in strength and ferocity.

Just as I used to push my explorations further and further into the depths during the first days, so now I made more and more use of the hours before nightfall. The lower the sun sank, the more activity there seemed to be on the sea bed. Shoals of apparently unending extent streamed up from the deeper water; it often looked as though their individual members were shooting about in a kind of spasmodic dance; next, they would dart after the small organisms floating in the water. Slender, elongate mackerel scads, their gills inflated, tore past in silvery squadrons. The ghostly silhouettes of rhinoceros fish hung, by hundreds and thousands, against the dark spaces of the

Above the sea the sun was preparing to sink behind the clouds. Below the sea an enormous butterfly—a manta ray—swam round me in a wide arc, its eye fixed steadily upon me as it came closer and closer, its conspicuous horns curling and uncurling.

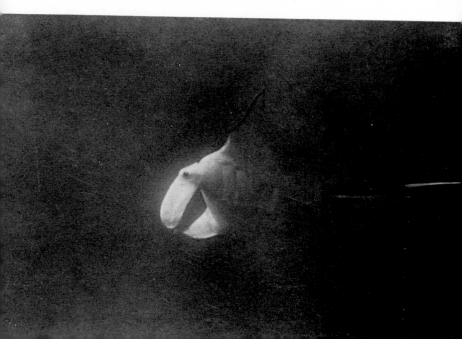

The keepers at the lonely lighthouse at Sanganeb gave us a friendly welcome. I made arrangements with them for the time when I should return with a full crew.

In the grottoes burrowed under the banks of sheer coral at Sanganeb I discovered this small, comic fish which I baptized "puffo" on account of its plump little stomach.

Such a spectacle I had never encountered before. In great sweeping
curves the mighty monster came circling right up to my camera!

At the railway station I photographed the swarm of white-robed figures who were about to board the tropical train for Khartoum.

Bill and I stopped before a façade of massive proportions. It was the Governor's Palace, resplendent with a new coat of whitewash, making it resemble a fairytale sugar-icing palace.

depths; and misshapen giant groupers drifted motionless, like buoys, in the open water.

The reefs themselves never showed up in such clear, decorative outlines as during these last hours of the day when a pallid moonlight would strip them of their gloomy veils. Yet I was overcome by dread more than once when I saw the great black rocks encircling me and realized where I was and in what circumstances. It was never sharks, however, that caused me to confess myself beaten and make my escape from the steadily increasing blackness of the night; actually, nothing looks lovelier or less menacing than a shark seen by night when he rises from the unknown depths, assumes visible shape, and goes gliding away in proud confidence through these darkling scenes. Rather the indistinctness of the water's black shadows, ready to give birth at any moment to some monstrous beast, inspired my deep foreboding.

One Thursday I accompanied the supply ship to Sanganeb, where the four lonely lighthouse keepers received me with cordial hospitality. The reefs at this spot dropped sheer for sixty feet, and deep grottoes burrowed under their banks. I spent the two hours of my stay almost entirely in these caverns, where I discovered a small fish, which I baptized, on account of his plump little stomach, as "puffo." He would have been a smash-hit as a comedian on any stage in the world. For some reason or other he was obsessed with the desire to bite his tiny tail, and the problem took so much of his attention that he had no time for anything else. First he would turn right, then left; then he would have a rest and start again.

The evening before my departure for Khartoum we were

sailing, just before sunset, alongside the Wingate Reef on our way home, when I caught sight of two delicate fin tips flitting playfully across the water with about fifteen feet between them. The monstrous beast again and just at the same spot! And this time the water was clear!

We hauled down the sail at once and approached, rowing cautiously. I inserted in the camera, as rapidly as I could, a particularly sensitive type of film, praying that I might still be in time. The sun was hovering on the upper margin of a black wall of cloud and would disappear into it during the next ten minutes and that would be the end of photography for that day.

As I slid overboard, the fins vanished under water. I swam in the direction I had last seen them. The sea was bottomless. The sun suddenly sank behind the clouds and everything became pitch-dark. But there was still a tiny window in the clouds, toward which the glowing sphere's light was making its way. When the feeble rays broke through, I might have two or three minutes of visibility.

I was swimming irresolutely in a circle when I saw movement on a large scale far to my left. It looked as though an enormous butterfly was fluttering about beneath the waves. At that moment the sun reached that rent in the clouds. I swam for all I was worth in the direction of the butterfly. It was, as I had already half suspected, a giant manta, in other words a ray called "the devil," on account of its conspicuous horns. I had not previously been aware that these monsters were to be found in the Red Sea; they are the largest of all known rays and may measure as much as twenty-two feet across and weigh six thousand pounds.

I never saw a creature, except certain playfully graceful

sharks, express such evident joy in being alive as did this beast. Heaving its tremendous flippers up and down—it was their extreme tips that had appeared alternately or simultaneously above the water—this "devil" was spinning in little circles and seemed as utterly absorbed in itself and its private delight as the Sanganeb "puffo" with its tail-chasing.

Then it caught sight of me.

It ceased to move. It turned. It looked at me. It became uneasy. Its projecting horns curled—then, with sudden determination, it came straight at me!

I forced myself to be calm, focused the camera. In the middle of the gigantic, swinging shape yawned a four-cornered opening: the mouth. Above at each side protruded the horns, stretched out stiff and straight. Halfway across the space between us, the monster turned suddenly and swam in a great semicircle around me, its eye staring fixedly at me as it spiraled closer and closer. It still seemed to be in good humor and kept wriggling its amazing horns.

These horns were, in fact, two thick lobes standing out right and left of the jaws and evidently served to close the latter, when required, in the fashion of a double door. But those great jaws created a misconception: despite its enormous size the manta is harmless and feeds, like many whales, on tiny floating marine organisms. Diminutive shrimps and sea snails were the tidbits for which this giant butterfly was lying in wait. If the manta, as I learned later, is hated and feared by fishermen, such feelings are based upon a misunderstanding.

No creature in the world is so much devoted to tranquil enjoyment; yet tormenting animalculae are the manta's constant companions, especially at the inner side of the horns, where they cause itching. In order to get rid of this tiresome nuisance, the manta scratches himself in a manner of his own. When he passes a fishing smack anchored by a chain, he takes the latter gratefully between his horns and rubs against it till he has squashed all the troublesome parasites. Unfortunately, a by-product of this massage treatment is often the dragging of the anchor, which then ties itself round his head, with the result that he dashes off in a panic, taking the vessel itself with him. More than one fisherman has found himself in a serious situation owing to this behavior; so the manta, not simply because of his horns, but for other reasons too, is called "the devil."

I took one photograph after another, till the ray was so close to me that his flippers practically touched me. Just as the first manta I had seen, he gave a sudden start of fright. I was caught up into a violent whirlpool and sent spinning; the lean black streak of his tail slid past—and the sun went down. No stage manager ever timed his effect more precisely!

The next day, at four o'clock in the afternoon, Achmed drove us to the railway station, where a swarm of figures swathed in white were busy about a long train of white-painted carriages. Their windows were protected against the harsh glare of the desert by agreeably tinted neophane glass. We got in and the train started off for Khartoum, for the King's birthday. One of the passengers in our car was an elderly gentleman with a long gray beard. Bill introduced me to him.

"Mr. Milward," said he. "You will be interested to meet our diver."

Mr. Milward was interested in anything that had to do with the sea. I learned that he had written a brochure on the Dungunab pearl-fishing industry, which he said would fascinate me. He was emphatic that I should do some diving in the Dungunab area.

"It's another ten miles on from Muhammad Qol, where you still intend to go some time," Bill explained to me. "You'll also find there what's left of Dr. Crossland's Institute, which cost the government more money than five new schools would have done."

"But he may have only just had bad luck," Mr. Milward suggested. "Perhaps the Japanese only got in a few months ahead of him, after all. Who can tell?"

Dr. Crossland was an English biologist who, between 1905 and 1921, had been in charge of a pearl-fishing station near Dungunab, in desolate country. His investigations, which went on behind barbed wire, were concerned with the artificial culture of pearl mussels. He had been censured for reckless expenditure, involving considerable sums, on his researches. Finally the government put a stop to further work in this connection.

"He was a very good scientist," Bill sighed. "Died in Copenhagen in 1944."

"At what depth are the banks situated?" I asked.

"I don't know exactly," Bill answered. "But at any rate the natives don't go down further than you can see from the boat. Their technique is still the same as it was in the time of Mohammed. When the windless seasons come round, the boats cruise about till those aboard spot a mussel, then they go down and fetch it up. Formerly children were trained for the job. But we put a stop to that by decree."

"Do they find any pearls there?"

Bill yawned. "Soon I shall have been here twenty years, but I don't know any more about it than you do. At the auctions there's never anything to see but the mussels; the pearls are dealt with 'under the table.' Two years ago, when I was going on leave, I had two of the finest pearls I have ever seen offered me. They were pear-shaped and both looked exactly alike; you could have made a magnificent pair of earrings out of them. I was offered them as a gift; but of course we're not allowed to take presents."

"I was once present at a deal in pearls," said Mr. Milward. "Even today the ceremony proceeds according to the ancient conventions. The two parties sit opposite each other at a table, clasp hands, and a cloth is laid across them. A third man acts as intermediary; one of the two dealers whispers the first bid into the intermediary's ear and he passes it on, in a whisper, to the second party. The consequence is that the dealer can see the other's reaction from his face and also feel it in his hands. If the bid is too low, the other draws his hand back, and if the bidder is prepared to go higher, he will keep hold of the other's hand with an almost imperceptible pressure of the fingertips.

"A hand which is sweating excessively toward the end of the deal may reveal that the owner sets particular store by the pearl, and this may result in the other breaking off negotiations and testing the market elsewhere. A rich American may be about who is looking for a counterpart to a certain pearl and is ready to pay any price for it. If the hand is withdrawn altogether, it indicates that negotiations are broken off; if it is held tight and shaken that means agreement."

We passed some camels which were lying on the ground with their hind legs tied together. When they saw the train, they jumped up in a panic and executed, despite their tethered condition, grotesque leaps in the air. A little later a red dot could be discerned on the desert. It consisted of a group of five women, tramping along in their red saris. As the train passed, they drew their veils over their heads and turned away.

Mr. Milward retired to his private compartment; Bill and I entered the dining car, where we sat until dinner time. Outside there were fewer bushes in the desert now and the ground was becoming rocky. In the fast gathering twilight we could still see the jagged peaks of the first range of hills. Then it grew quite dark. Bill told me that all this district was full of baboons. Before we went to bed, he advised me to close the window of my compartment, for people at the stations, he said, had long rods with which they "fished" plunder out of the carriages.

"Did you see the ostriches?" was his first question next morning.

"No, I didn't see anything," I replied. Achmed hadn't come to wake me, and it was half-past nine by the time I opened my eyes.

The landscape was now altogether different. The mountains lay far behind us, and we were crossing a desert devoid of trees, shrubs, stones of any size, and in fact any noticeable object at all. It was an apparently endless, utterly flat plain, which stretched, like a sea, to the very horizon.

We stopped at a few watchmen's huts here and there, where old women ran alongside the train and offered for sale cucumbers no thicker than one's finger and tiny ears of roasted corn. Such was the most the soil could produce in this desolate part of the country. Further on, we passed isolated, barren trees and some hills that resembled towering, artificially piled heaps of rubble. At last a green streak could be discerned in the distance; these were the fertile, cultivated banks of the Nile.

At a fairly large station I watched a dignified Arab being greeted by his wives; each kissed his hand respectfully.

I rang for the guard, to order ice water. But no one came. So in the end I went to look for the man myself. He had spread himself a carpet at the end of the car, in a corner, and was saying his prayers on it.

"In two weeks we shall be celebrating the Feast of the Prophet," Bill said, as we stood together at the window. "There will be great doings in Port Sudan. The faithful assemble outside the town, praying and dancing about and repeating the name of Allah hundreds and thousands of times, till many of them go into absolute trances and fall down. The day before yesterday I got a letter from the Grand Cadi requesting me to make sure that there is no drinking or playing of games, and above all that the sexes do not intermingle."

Small boats, heavily laden, drifted on the sluggish waters of the Nile. In a large cornfield we saw a little boy standing on a small mound of earth, with three strings in his hand. Each of the strings stretched, over a considerable distance, to a separate pole from which a tin receptacle dangled, filled with stones. If a bird settled anywhere in the field, the boy scared it by rattling the tin nearest the intruder.

"That's the kind of job I've always longed for," observed Bill dreamily.

It was quite dark by the time we finally reached Khartoum. A friend of Bill's picked us up at the station in his car; Bill was to stay with him, and a room had been booked for me in the Grand Nile Hotel. They dropped me there. The place resembled the Red Sea Hotel but was a good deal bigger.

I was still sitting in my bath when Bill called. He said he was terribly sorry, but the party to which he had been invited consisted of twelve people and the hostess wouldn't hear of there being thirteen people at the table. Unfortunately, they hadn't been able to find a lady for me, to make fourteen. He had decided to decline the invitation and spend the evening with me.

I begged him earnestly not to bother about me. I was dead tired and would be only too delighted to put my evening clothes back in the trunk. I finally convinced him.

Next morning Bill called for me at eleven o'clock, and we had lunch at his friend's house. Then a state coach, upholstered in red plush, appeared and we were driven away in it.

Everywhere in the streets it was obvious that something special was going on. The houses, for the most part of one story, were gaily beflagged. Khartoum had a much more European atmosphere than Port Sudan. There were modern shopping districts, and we passed imposing buildings, surrounded by large, well-kept gardens. We stopped before a façade of massive proportions. It was the palace of the Governor-General.

I followed Bill into the entrance hall, where weapons hung on the walls, and our cards of invitation were subjected to a strict scrutiny. We crossed a forecourt and reached the park, from which we had a view of the palace in all its splendor. It looked as if it had been made of sugar icing. Bill remarked, somewhat prosaically, that it had been given a new coat of whitewash since the last rains.

In the park, on a broad level lawn, flanked by two glorious royal palms, buffet tables stood in a wide semicircle, open on the palace side; and within the arc thus formed a great number of little tables, overspread with gaily striped umbrellas, and several rows of chairs were set out. Regretfully I had been obliged, at Bill's request, to leave my camera in the cloakroom. We mingled with the other guests. Those who held official rank appeared in bright uniforms and gorgeous robes of state, while the ordinary citizens who had been invited wore light suits and dark ties, and the English ladies, just as at the Epsom race track, were dressed in flowing summer frocks and big hats. The Sudanese chieftains came with rings on their feet and through their noses and were decked out in full regalia. The representatives of the Coptic Church displayed splendid chains hung across their stately paunches.

Bill seemed to know everybody. He talked to the chieftains as if they were old school friends of his, and the dignitaries greeted him with the greatest cordiality. He talked English to some, Arabic or a Sudanese dialect to others; he introduced me to all of them and told them all what I was doing. I was even introduced to the Commander-in-Chief, a general. Then we went over to a native chieftain, whose haughty, bellicose countenance was surmounted by crisp, reddish-gold curls.

"That was an old friend of mine," said Bill as soon as he

had introduced me and talked to him a little. "They get their hair that color by smearing it with cow dung."

Although delicious tidbits were piled high on the buffet tables around us, scarcely anyone except Bill had yet tasted them. Everyone seemed to be waiting, under strict discipline, for an event to take place. Finally, at a precisely determined instant it happened. To a great flourish of trumpets and the first part of the British national anthem, His Excellency the British Governor-General, with his consort at his side and numerous retinue, made his appearance. His entourage remained standing at the top of the open staircase that led down to the lawn, and there then ensued, while we all stood up to watch, a ceremonious and prolonged distribution of decorations. The first to receive their Orders were the English, among whom was a woman who had earned hers by Red Cross work; then came the Sudanese in uniform, very stiff and soldierly; others followed in civilian dress, who also saluted upon the receipt of their decorations. It was a relief when we saw the last members of the long line come up.

But the high light of the festive proceedings was still to come. His Excellency stepped forward, uniform ablaze with decorations, and delivered a solemn but quite inaudible address. The place where he was standing was too far away and a light wind carried his words into the bushes on either side of him. But the impression made was none the worse for that. On the contrary, the circumstance enabled one to concentrate on the actual result of the ceremony, which was the leisurely observation of the official representative of a mighty empire, framed in the dignified setting of the sugar-icing palace. Between him and ourselves, who stood below at some distance from him, yawned the gulf with which England invariably confronts the peoples over which she rules. It is true, however, that His Excellency, in conformity with modern taste, afterward descended the steps and made a long series of detours among his guests, every one of whom he greeted.

As we were standing rather far back, we had to be patient a little longer. At last it was our turn. His Excellency asked Bill why he had kept so modestly in the rear, then he shook hands with me and said, "Your work must be extremely interesting. But it is dangerous, too, is it not?"

I was about to reply when I perceived that no answer was expected. His Excellency had already turned to the next in the row, to whom he was speaking Arabic and who, like myself, did not get to the stage of replying. As over three hundred persons were present, the tour must have called for prodigious powers of endurance and concentration.

Behind His Excellency the ranks were breaking up and everyone joined the flow, under the compulsion of appetite, to the buffets. As the Sudanese are particularly addicted to sweets, the tidbits of this nature were soon diminished— Copts, chieftains, and ladies competing in the feast to their hearts' content.

"We shall have a strenuous day tomorrow," said Bill, as soon as we had taken our fill of sandwiches and sweets. "We are invited to breakfast with Sir Sayed Abdel Rahman, the Mahdi Pasha, and to lunch with His Excellency at the palace. For dinner we shall visit a real Sudanese at home. And we shall end up by relaxing from our exertions at Toni's, where there will be a party." He uttered a sigh, but whether one of pleasure at the anticipation of so many festivities or of melancholy at the prospect of the efforts they would necessarily demand, was not very clear. From previous observation of Bill I was inclined to believe the former.

"Very good!" I exclaimed, echoing Bill's favorite expression.

"Personally," he went on, "I shall also have to attend a school fete in the afternoon. But I know that wouldn't amuse you, so I said you wouldn't be able to come, though you were invited as well as myself."

"Very good!" I repeated, with even greater fervor.

The buffets were cleared of their burdens and the guests gradually dispersed. We drove back to the hotel and drank a few more rounds in private to the health of our recent host. Then Bill's friend drove us to the only cabaret in Khartoum for dinner. Here, in the open air, which was rather cold, some Hungarian girls gave an exhibition of African ballet dancing. Mindful of the day we had before us, we soon departed from this restaurant.

At eight o'clock the next morning Bill called for me in a car. Sir Sayed Abdel Rahman, the Mahdi Pasha, was said to be the wealthiest man in the Sudan. As the son of the great Mahdi, who had led a revolt against the Egyptian Government and captured Khartoum in 1885, he was the religious head of some ten thousand Mohammedans who considered it an honor to work, unpaid, in his extensive cotton fields. The fact that in these circumstances his annual income totaled five to eight million dollars was not to be wondered at.

We drove into a carefully kept garden and stopped in front of a palace built in the modern oriental style. Two attendants opened the door of the car and conducted us to an apartment on the ground floor, furnished in the old-fashioned way, where Sir Sayed Abdel Rahman—"The Mahdi" for short—awaited us, seated on a sofa one's grandmother might have used. He was a man of imposing presence, whose massive yet well-shaped features indicated intelligence and charity, though at the same time the ruthless inflexibility of an Eastern potentate. Although he was undoubtedly over sixty, his movements as he rose and greeted us were those of a mere lad. He was swathed in a dazzlingly white, flowing caftan and wore a turban adorned with jewels. In the fashion of the country, he bowed, touching forehead and chest, then invited us to be seated.

Bill explained my activities to the Mahdi, then interpreted the latter's reply, which was to this effect: He regretted that he spoke no English and though he knew something about horses and birds, he knew nothing about fish. In order to make some sort of answer, I asked Bill to tell him I had already heard of his magnificent horses. Back came, in a flash, the rejoinder that the Mahdi was extremely sorry that he had caught cold, otherwise he would have been delighted to show me the horses.

We passed into an adjoining apartment, the great dining room—a mirrored hall in Louis Quatorze style—and sat down at a lavishly laid table. It included large grapefruits from the host's own estate placed in silver dishes, the dishes flanked by tall, slender glasses of orange juice, dates, and a fruit with a lot of black pips, unfamiliar to me. The attendants then served—probably ministering to Bill's English palate—cornflakes with sugar and cream in soup plates, fried fish cutlets with sliced tomato and small lemons, and an omelette containing small pieces of chopped liver, with which we ate toast, butter, marmalade, and honey—the latter, very appropriately, from a silver bee, with its raised wings beaten to a delicate fragility.

During the meal the Mahdi described a water nymph which had been caught in the Nile when he was a boy. She had gotten entangled in a net not far from the place where he lived and had died in a few hours. Bill passed on to me the Mahdi's inquiry whether I had ever come across such a maiden in the sea. When I replied in the negative, the Mahdi went on to observe that the phenomenon was by no means uncommon in the Nile.

Finally the Mahdi showed us over his palace. The furniture included precious carpets as well as modern steel tables and chairs, and cheap prints cheek by jowl with artistic treasures of considerable value. In his bedroom he called our attention to a glass case containing fine specimens of goldsmiths' work and costly scarabs. The centerpiece was a splendid diamond. He had bestowed, so he told us, an even larger one on Princess Elizabeth, now Queen Elizabeth II.

Over coffee, which was served to us in the study, Bill and the Mahdi engaged in a long discussion, which was in all probability the real reason for our visit. I sat and listened politely, without understanding a single word. As the leader of the party of independence supported by the English, Sir Sayed Abdel Rahman, the Mahdi Pasha, occupied a central position in political life. When we finally took our leave, we found a group of dignitaries already waiting for an audience in the hall below.

Punctually at midday we entered the palace of the Governor-General and this time were conducted up to the second floor, where our hostess, Lady Howe, received us in amicable fashion. Soon afterward her husband appeared, accompanied by two adjutants and the Governor of Aden, and we passed into a lofty gallery—the dining hall—where a number of dark oil paintings gazed down upon us. The menu was exactly the same as that in Bill's own house, except that here the fried fish and roast mutton were followed by some very nice apple fritters and finally by a cheese so tough that we were obliged to cut the merest wisps from it. I sat on His Excellency's right, and the conversation swung to my diving activities.

Over coffee on the terrace he examined the submarine photographs I had brought with me, and I took the opportunity to mention to him my idea of an expedition on a larger scale. After a few questions His Excellency said I might rely upon his support. I could forward my application for visas for the various members of the expedition direct to him and in connection with the Customs formalities must enclose a detailed inventory of all the equipment and implements we should bring. He would then be prepared to recommend prompt dispatch of the articles. He shook hands with me very cordially when we took our leave.

That evening Bill and I, in evening dress, entered an apartment of considerable length, with more resemblance to the oriental style of a cheap suburban theater than to what I had expected of the dining room of a prosperous Sudanese. The walls were hung with pictures painted upon cloth and stained-glass windows surmounted the front door. To the right, behind the long table set for dinner, stood a sideboard, and behind a screen there was a cheap washstand. To the left, at the back of the room, several Sudanese were seated on broad divans at small Turkish tables, smoking hookahs.

After we had waited rather a long time for the last of the guests to arrive, we sat down to dinner. There was thin soup, with pieces of bread floating in it, then some fish mayonnaise which tasted neither of fish nor of mayonnaise, and finally roast mutton, which was set on the table in the form of a single joint, from which our host carved large slices, subsequently laying them on his guests' plates. After four weeks in the Sudan I flattered myself I was something of a connoisseur of mutton, but this specimen was by far the toughest I had ever had between my jaws. The last course was a synthetic fruit jelly. As, in addition to all this, I didn't understand a word of the lively conversation going on, I was only too pleased to find myself in the street again with all my teeth still in my head.

"In the ordinary way the Sudanese eat with their hands," Bill explained to me, as we drove off in the car. "The host makes a dumpling out of rice and gravy, by kneading it, and pops it into his respected guest's mouth."

"What about Toni?" I asked.

"Toni isn't a bit like that," Bill informed me soothingly. "He's a Greek and his parties are the best in the Sudan. He owns all the cinemas and knows how to spend money like a gentleman. By the way, two of the highest Sudanese officials in the government were our fellow guests just now."

We stopped at a house from which dance music and the laughter of women resounded. Through the door we could see a small bar, at which our host was just then entertaining some ladies. As soon as he saw Bill, he spread out his arms and came to meet us as if he trod on air, a happy condition which I at first attributed to the champagne bottle he was carrying, but later realized was inborn exuberance.

We had glasses pressed into our hands and were soon a part of the frivolous crowd. Dancing was going on in the moonlit garden among the flowering shrubs; on the way there you came across a buffet loaded with suckling pigs, lobsters, and caviar, in addition to the most exquisite Greek dainties. Bill and I exchanged gloomy looks, remembering how we had stuffed our insides with tough mutton and synthetic fruit jelly. Toni was an ideal host. He bobbed up wherever there was an empty glass or a conversation at a dead end.

At six in the morning I was dragged out of bed by one of the hotel servants. At half-past seven Bill and I were climbing aboard the little plane that served travelers to the coast. By half-past nine we had made up our lost sleep and were already circling over Port Sudan.

Below us rolled the sulfur-yellow clouds of a sandstorm. Here and there open spaces were still visible which showed indistinct traces of the ground, but they soon shifted their positions and grew noticeably smaller. We heard later that the pilot had almost made up his mind to return to Khartoum. He described three great circles above the town, then decided to chance it, and down we went through the last opening. The moment the machine had landed our environment changed to a yellowish-gray fog.

Out of the wall of mist came Achmed, the chauffeur, and a police officer, who gave Bill his report in the car. At home we breakfasted, then Bill took his brief case and went off to the office.

"Back to the mill again," he observed, without enthusiasm. His spirits had sunk to zero once more.

PEARL BANKS

PEARL BANKS

I SAT IN MY BATH and read the numerous letters which had finally caught up with me. Lotte seemed very worried; she had managed to get hold of a new Leica, but an export permit was proving hard to obtain. And in addition to that, she wrote that nothing had been heard from me for three weeks and people were already saying I was dead. A letter from a newspaper asked for an immediate report from me. An agency announced that it was not prepared to advance me any money. My family begged me, for heaven's sake, to drop them a line. A friend wrote to say that another friend had gotten married. But the most interesting item was a parcel from Mr. Milward, which contained a book by Dr. Crossland and his own brochure about the pearl banks at Dungunab.

I read it with growing interest. When I had finished it, I knew that I positively had to do some diving there. I immediately began to make all the necessary preparations for a journey to Muhammad Qol. Four days later I was sitting with Mahmud on a heavily laden truck, rumbling out of Port Sudan.

Mahmud was swathed in an enormous white robe which, as I was to learn later, was intended to serve not only as attire for the occasion but also, at night, as a bed. As he sat there, high up on the piles of luggage, and stared haughtily into the wind of our progress, I was sure that his thoughts were busy with an incident, extremely disagreeable to him personally, of which I had been a witness some days before.

We had gone out sailing, and I had been surprised to find that we were using a different felucca and that O Sheik was not present. Mahmud dismissed my inquiries about O Sheik with a gesture that might have meant either that he was dead or that he had gotten married. When we returned to harbor again, a crowd of people was awaiting us.

The central figure in the serried ranks on the quay revealed itself, as we drew nearer, to be an extraordinarily stout Arab whose massive hulk was swathed in gorgeous robes. To my astonishment Mahmud put the helm over and steered for another part of the harbor, where we had never landed before.

"What's the matter? What's the meaning of this?" I asked Mahmud, by signs. He gave me to understand, in a flood of explanatory phrases, that there was nothing whatever to worry about. I gave him instructions to land at the usual place. Thereupon he made me a lengthy speech to the effect that it was no good going there, as the people ashore were not quite in their right senses. It was far better to do what we were doing.

Then I ordered him, peremptorily, to land where we always landed. While we were still bearing down on the quay, Mahmud assailed the stout stranger with a bombardment of short phrases. He then hurriedly made the boat fast and sprang ashore, where he addressed the stout and gorgeously clad Arab with vehement gesticulations, while the latter's features showed every sign of indignation.

I found the whole thing too ridiculous. I called to Mahmud, telling him to get my things out of the boat and follow me to the house. I didn't at all care for the looks of the staring multitude.

"I are interpreter," a dwarfish little fellow stated, pushing his way to the front and approaching me.

Mahmud seized him and hurled him aside. The stout man now lost his temper and grabbed Mahmud from behind. Mahmud let out a yell of distress and tried to fight him off. I was only just in time, by resolutely getting between them, to prevent a general hand-to-hand scuffle, in which Mahmud would certainly have gotten the worst of it.

The would-be interpreter was so frightened that the little English he knew had deserted him. I managed to reassure him and gradually discovered, in the intervals of Mahmud's interruptions, what the matter was.

The stout man was the owner of our former felucca, and he indignantly stated that he had been cheated. I had been in the habit of handing Mahmud, every evening, the combined fee for the use of the boat and its crew of two; but all of my payments had gone into Mahmud's pocket and stayed there. Mahmud declared that he had needed the money, of which only a small part was due to him personally, as a loan for the purchase of medicine for his sick wife. The stout man contended, on the other hand, that Mahmud had bought the new boat with the money. After assuring the Arab that I would investigate the matter, I left the quay with Mahmud in tow.

"He's just a rascal," said Bill, when I told him about this affair. "Of course he bought a boat for himself with the money, but we'll soon put the matter straight."

Mahmud was standing there watching us with a serious and intent expression, like that of a magistrate. I was worried about the business, for Mahmud was absolutely essential to me for the journey to Muhammad Qol.

Bill had a talk with him, then turned to me and said Mahmud would repay the money. The wealthy ship owner, Mahmud had added further, was a man without charity, who sucked the blood of the poor and would assuredly end up in the scorching desert of damnation. In order to avoid any further misunderstanding, I requested Bill to ask Mahmud to state his fee for the journey to Muhammad Qol.

Mahmud's face cleared and he spoke for five minutes without a break.

"What did he say?" I demanded.

"I couldn't possibly translate all of it to you," Bill answered. "The long and short of it is, that you and he are brothers and that one doesn't charge a brother anything. Five pounds [$14] and his food will be enough. But don't forget you'll have to be back by Saturday, as there'll be a dance at the club that night. Don't you remember that Saturday is Christmas Eve?"

Christmas in six days! The scorching desert we were crossing made the date incredible. As I was being too much shaken about at the back of the truck, I made it stop and got in beside the driver. In spite of the side draft caused by our forward motion, it was so hot in the driver's compartment that the sweat ran off me in streams.

We drove north along the coast, then turned inland toward the mountains. The road, which was not too bad, followed the course of the Port Sudan water supply. The Sodom apple bushes were left behind and the acacia trees, with their flat branch patterns, so characteristic of the African steppe country, grew more frequent. At the foot of the hills we came upon a river that still had water in it, owing to the recent heavy rains. The stream, however, had gotten so shallow that we could cross its broad, stony bottom by boldly zigzagging.

The driver, a Negro, was an expert at his trade. He did the run to an outpost every week with foodstuffs, and we had contracted with him to take us as far as Muhammad Qol, halfway to his destination, and to pick us up four days later for the return journey.

The landscape now changed continually. We drove across lumpy hillsides, strewn with boulders, over areas of volcanic rock, then through a sandy desert in which we negotiated, with astounding dexterity, a couple of lofty dunes at full throttle. When we got further into the hills, the road became edged with fields of cactus, and in a few level places, lightly covered with green vegetation, camels were feeding, watched over by nomads. We also passed some solitary nomads, but didn't meet a single motor vehicle.

At midday, halfway to our destination, we came to a small village of extremely primitive dwellings, made of stones and interlaced branches, and drove past a fountain where two girls were watering a few goats. One of the young women was nude to the waist and both face and figure made a charming impression. I remembered for a long time, as we drove on, the majestic grace with which she unhurriedly raised her upper garment to veil herself. In the brief glance she threw me could be read all the pride and barbaric wildness of the nomadic inhabitants of this immense desert. They had not the faintest interest in what might be happening in the great world beyond. This was their home, where they lived completely self-reliant lives, surrounded by an implacable environment, from which they wrung their subsistence. The men, too, whom we passed, regarded us proudly, with a clear and direct gaze.

The sun sank lower. The savage mountain country we were traversing seemed endless, and all my muscles were aching from the continuous jolting. Mahmud, on his high perch, resembled a white pillar: his flowing draperies left only his eyes visible. It grew dark and the road began to slope gradually downhill. At last, two hours after sunset, we reached Muhammad Qol.

We stopped at an old fort that stood in the desert like a single block of white stone. From the wretched wooden hovels surrounding it isolated lights gleamed through the chinks of the ill-fitting planks which formed their walls. Our headlights illuminated a second, somewhat smaller truck. Chattering natives, carrying small lamps, came running toward us. I alighted and stretched; then a stout, arrogant-looking Fuzzy in uniform presented himself. I handed him a document which Bill had given me, addressed to the *Omda,* the highest ranking of all the Fuzzies, in case the latter happened to be in Muhammad Qol. The uniformed man indicated the direction in which, far, far away, the *Omda* was just then in residence. He himself was Omar Effendi, the head man of this flower of cities.

I didn't like the fellow. Just then we were joined by a fat Sudanese with an amiable countenance, like a full moon, surmounted by a white, nightcap-shaped headgear. He invited me to enter the fort. Mahmud, meanwhile, gave orders for the luggage to be unloaded and signed to me not to worry.

The interior of the fort was composed of a series of kennel-like apartments, where a couple of Sudanese soldiers had set up their camp beds. We climbed a narrow wooden staircase to the roof. Here a central structure stood, consisting of two small rooms separated by a passage. The man with the nightcap, who spoke a little English, told me that one of these was at my disposal. There was only one small table and a chair in it. The other room, which looked quite comfortable, was where he himself lived.

He invited me to drink some tea with him and included the uncongenial Effendi, who immediately installed himself in the only decent armchair. In a long and difficult conversation the Sudanese tried to explain to me what he was doing at the fort. Finally it dawned on me that by the word, "locust," which he repeated continually, he meant "grasshopper." He was an official of the Grasshopper Control Service, and traveled up and down the coast to report the appearance of grasshoppers anywhere in his district.

With the most helpful assiduity he interpreted my questions to a lean old fisherman who had been called in and was now standing motionless in the doorway like a death's-head at a carnival. The island of Mayetib was very well known to everyone about here, and it seemed that sharks were to be found there in vast numbers. Meanwhile Mahmud had stowed our gear in the other room; he, too, came to join in the conversation and started reciting the saga of our adventures together. The uncongenial Effendi now became almost friendly. He rose, and after a time came back with a bowl of steaming rice, which he placed before me on the table with his own hands.

After I had eaten some of it with suitable courtesy, I inquired where I could wash. Almost at once two soldiers dragged a tin bathtub, half-full, into my room, and I cleaned myself up in it, with the greatest delight, from top to toe. Mahmud had already set up the camp bed Bill had given me to take along and had most obligingly placed my slippers beside it. Though the night was rather windy, he insisted on sleeping out in the open, on the roof. To this I agreed and lent him one of my blankets.

By the light of a small oil lamp I examined some old maps and visitors' books which I found in the drawer of the table. Then I made all the necessary preparations for the next day. My first objective, though Mahmud and all the rest strongly advised against it, was Mayetib, where the Governor had seen such a lot of sharks. The old fisherman, to whom the only felucca in the place belonged, had orders to have the boat ready by six in the morning. It was to sail with the first blush of dawn.

Before I lay down, I went for a stroll, still in slippers, among the scattered hovels, from which obscure sounds reached me. The immense tent of the sky, spangled with innumerable stars, spread over the tiny village. There were not more than forty huts in all, which were collected, like stray sheep, all round the fort. To one side lay the unbroken plain of the desert, on the other the sea, glittering in the starlight, with a small pier projecting into it.

At six in the morning Mahmud came to wake me with a cup of tea and I was soon ready. By daylight our surroundings looked even more cheerless. Though I could see right across the desert to the mountain ranges, which must have been over six thousand feet high, the sea was covered by an impenetrable mist. The boat, a considerably smaller felucca than the one in Port Sudan, was already waiting for us. Mahmud and the old fisherman stowed our belongings aboard and we started off.

A very light offshore breeze carried us over the smooth, mirror-like surface of the water. The coast and the fort gradually fell further behind us and ahead the first outlines of the large island of Mukawwar began to appear out of the mist. We set a course which would leave the island to one side of us. As daylight increased, a cone became visible behind the island, far away on the horizon. According to Mahmud, that was Mayetib. He added that the wind was unfavorable; if we really wanted to sail so far, it would be impossible for us to get back by the evening and we should have to spend the night there.

"All right, in that case we will spend the night there," was my reply to this objection.

Neither Mahmud nor the fisherman seemed much gratified at this decision. Instead of holding a direct course for the cone, Mahmud steered steadily for the open sea. In reply to my protests he gave an explanation which I could not understand. Bill had described an atoll to me, excellent for fishing, which lay further out to sea: I thought that perhaps the two men wanted to take me there. Accordingly, I asked Mahmud whether the place we were bound for was a straight reef or a ring. He answered that it was straight, but that we would sail round it in a circle. After that, I gave up.

Mukawwar and Mayetib fell further and further away on our quarter and I got angrier and angrier. We passed a reef with an extraordinary top to it, then suddenly Mahmud brought the boat about sharply, and we started on a direct course for the little cone. I had misjudged him. He had not mutinied at all. We had simply been obliged to sail round an extensive reef area.

There was something puzzling about that distant cone. Though we now had the wind behind us and our worm-eaten little craft was skimming over the waves toward it like a bird, we didn't seem to get any nearer and it didn't seem to get any bigger. It glided ahead of us like an unattainable phantom.

On the other hand, the towering cliffs of Mukawwar grew more and more massive as we approached. Although I was sure it was merely an optical illusion, I began to wonder whether I myself had not made a complete mistake and the Governor had been talking, not of Mayetib, but of Mukawwar. The sea hereabout did not seem to be more than sixty feet deep anywhere. Looking down from the bow I could see the sandy bottom quite clearly, crisscrossed by a great number of walls of reef.

The sun had already reached the zenith when we finally beached our craft on the snow-white sands of the phantom island. It comprised a cone of rock, 125 or 150 feet high, towering in solitary state not far from a reef that ran as straight as a tape measure. Hundreds of crabs fled in all directions as I jumped ashore. Screaming sea birds circled above my head as I clambered up the rocks to the crest of the cone. One bird, which clearly had its nest in the vicinity, came within six feet of me, shrieking loudly and flapping its wings wildly, with a fish, still alive, in its talons.

From the top of the island I gazed out over the sea in all directions. The adjoining reef, running toward the open sea, was precipitous, but over toward the island of Mukawwar an apparently endless series of flat sandbanks stretched away. It was certainly possible that the Governor had seen plenty of sharks here; all the same, there wasn't one in sight at the moment. On the other hand, I did notice something else which interested me quite as much. The reef suddenly came to an end some distance away, then started again, in a straight line as before, a little further on, thus forming a wide gateway leading from the open sea into the broad, flat maritime area lying between the two islands. No doubt there were strong currents running in and out there. Conditions must be exceptionally favorable, therefore, for the growth of corals.

Rapidly I scrambled down the rocks to the shore and found Mahmud making a careful search of the sands. Then he threw a handline, in a wide arc, into the shallows, where a number of dark shapes could be dimly seen glimmering below the surface. The bait had hardly smacked down into the water before he began to haul in vigorously. I saw the dark shapes shooting about in a frenzy and a big fish in the middle of them thrashing about wildly at the surface. Mahmud had soon pulled him into the shallow water and played him to a standstill. It was a bayard weighing a good sixteen pounds.

Mahmud declared that it was not worth while stepping the mast to cover the short distance to the opening in the reef. He and the old man rowed the boat to that point, where two currents met, forming a whirl of eddies. The whole of my experience in the Caribbean meant nothing if that were not a particularly interesting place to dive—and full of sharks in the bargain.

I climbed overboard and looked down. Fire coral was here predominant on the sea bed. Its hundreds of fantastically curved and branching slabs formed a collection of tall, saffron-yellow trunks, and close by, near a smooth wall of rock, hovered a great number of small and somewhat larger fish, all their heads turned in the same direction, lashing away with their tails as they struggled against the strong current.

I dived and took some photographs, but each time I reached the bottom I found that the current had swept me a good distance off my course. So I fought my way forward to the outermost corner of the gateway and slipped sideways into the shadow on the current cast by the reef. Deep inlets had been formed here by the vigorous agitation of the water and they broadened into lagoons in the interior of the reef.

The sea bed, thirty-five to forty-five feet down, was overgrown with exceedingly luxuriant corals, gorgeously colored; they showed clearly the influence of the currents, which continually carried in fresh alimentary particles. There was also a superabundance of fish. Spotted spiny-rayed perch and whole troops of big groupers swam to and fro between the

On our drive from Port Sudan to Muhammad Qol we passed a solitary desert nomad, astride a camel. We also came to a village where primitive dwellings were made of stones and interlaced branches.

The old fort at Muhammad Qol stood in the desert like a cube of white stone, and wretched wooden hovels surrounded it on all sides.

Against the fort I posed a group of natives. "Uncle Locusts" told me their diet consisted chiefly of dried dates.

"Uncle Locusts," the friendly Sudanese whom I met at Muhammad Qol and who accompanied me to Dungunab.

From behind, a giant of a shark, at least twelve feet long, appeared..... He changed his position and charged me at full speed.

Mahmud beached our craft on a sandbank to await the return of the mantas.

I retrieved this fiddle-shaped creature from the sandy bottom with my bare hands. It is a halavi, a queer sort of link between a shark and a skate.

gaily hued beds. I had never before seen such great shoals of blue surgeonfish as here. From the cavities between the corals the long feelers of rock lobsters kept watch. A little further on I met three small sharks, which thereafter followed me about like faithful dogs. Lower down, where the rock fell away, two bigger ones were swimming, which I only recognized at first from their white fin tips, as they flitted along in the gloom of the deeper water. Unfortunately the sun was just then veiled by scattered clouds, so the scene was not sufficiently distinct for photographing.

Later on the two sharks rose higher and I saw to my astonishment that each of them was accompanied by a mackerel. One had a blue mackerel, the other a yellow one. The mackerel kept close to the dorsal fins of the sharks and imitated their every movement. I had already made a similar observation in the Caribbean but then had supposed it to have been a unique exception. Probably the mackerel shared, somehow or other, the sharks' meals; but why the latter tolerated the presence of these smaller predatory fish I couldn't understand.

Regretfully, an hour later, I climbed back into the boat. If we still wanted to get back to Muhammad Qol before nightfall, it was high time to depart. I should have liked to spend a month at this place alone. All the same, I shouldn't have cared to harpoon a fish at the spot where the rock fell away. The result would probably have been a gathering of sharks from which I doubt if I should have escaped with a whole skin.

We had scarcely left Mayetib behind us—we were making a wide sweep out into the open sea—when two big porpoises turned up and accompanied the boat, playing about all the time. After three-quarters of an hour we tacked and ran at full speed before the wind toward an endless white line that seemed to have been drawn across the sea with a ruler. Mahmud handed me the satchel containing my clothes, camera, and tropical helmet, indicating that I was to hold it above my head. He was making, in a dead straight line, for the reef. We seemed to bob for a moment, then rose in the air; a breaker grabbed us from behind, hurled us onward; we banged once more against the coral in the shallows; then we had passed over the wall! Mahmud had saved at least an hour by this maneuver, for otherwise we should have had to dodge right round the whole reef against the wind.

"You wouldn't have done that if it had been your felucca, you rascal!" I told him.

He shook his head, grinning delightedly from ear to ear. The unfortunate fisherman to whom the boat belonged had been cowering at the bottom of the craft in a panic, hoping for the best. Compared with the exuberant personality of Mahmud, his was merely that of a bruised violet.

It was already growing dark when a fin bobbed up close by and I sprang into the water. But there was nothing to be seen anywhere except tiny sea snails, fluttering through the water like gnats. Mahmud now began to make jokes about sleeping on Mukawwar and eating raw fish. But it was already evident that we should be back in Muhammed Qol before night set in.

All the local notabilities were waiting for us on the pier as we came alongside. That avuncular personage, the locust research man, had already been worrying about us. Omar Effendi wanted to hear about the sharks and later on, when

Mahmud was frying our bayard, he again brought in a big bowl of rice. I was asked whether I would like another bath, but this time I felt I could dispense with that luxury. Fresh water was a rarity here—it had to be brought in from the mountains, a day's journey away, in leather bottles. I told "Uncle Locusts" about my intention to dive at Dungunab the following day, and he advised me to send the boat over there very early in the morning, after which he would drive me overland to the spot. He was going to pay a visit to Dungunab in any case, so we could easily kill two birds with one stone.

I woke up about eight the next morning. As we were not going to start until ten o'clock, I could take it easy until then. When I shouted, Mahmud appeared with the tea. He placed the cup, the pot, and the sugar on the small chest that contained our provisions and pushed it over to the head of my bed.

When he had left the room, I picked up the tray, to get some marmalade and biscuits out of the chest, and a tiny mouse suddenly jumped—almost into my face! It raced across the room like lightning and disappeared into the corner where the harpoon stood. It took refuge behind the shaft, with only its whiskers showing round one side of it.

I left it there and got my biscuit; then I nearly dropped my cup. A second tiny mouse had popped up, again almost in my face. It dashed across the room, found the other, and both vanished through a crack under the door. I had forgotten that mice were prevalent in the desert!

As I breakfasted in bed, I reread the passage in Dr. Crossland's book about the pearl banks. Then I got the old map

227

from the table drawer and studied the layout of the many coral reefs that crisscrossed the sea in the vicinity of Muhammad Qol. The furthest extremity of this vast area of reefs was marked by the atoll Bill had told me about. Its ring was fairly large, broken at several places and just about as far from Muhammad Qol as the island of Mayetib.

According to Darwin's theory, atolls were originally the barrier reefs of islands which gradually sank into the sea, while the reefs grew steadily higher, so that finally only the coral ring remained above the surface. In the case of this atoll such an origin seemed hardly credible; the water inside the ring was too deep for that. A special feature of interest was a tiny island in the middle of the ring. If the map had been correctly drawn, it rose from the depths like a slender, perpendicular tower. I had already noticed, from the aircraft, pointed reefs of this shape on the Arabian coast. I decided that this island should be my goal on the third day.

We drove out of Muhammad Qol soon after ten o'clock. Omar Effendi, too, insisted on accompanying us. The desert grew more and more desolate, till at last it was nothing but sand. We saw some gazelles in the distance, then we passed a number of skeletons, bleached white, which were lying near the road, half-buried in the sand which had blown over them. "Uncle Locusts'" driver was a phlegmatic sort of chap. Every four minutes the engine would stall, he would then get out and poke a long piece of wire into the works, always in the same slapdash kind of way, with the result that the engine would start up again for a short time.

The village of Dungunab was even more of a wretched hole than Muhammad Qol. There were only about half as many huts and these consisted of more chinks than wood.

Some fishermen greeted us with friendly handshakes. Even this tiny, isolated settlement provided a welcome for visitors. We were invited to enter the "Rest-Hut," consisting of one low-ceilinged room, with some camp beds standing against the wall. A special armchair was fetched for Omar Effendi.

Our felucca had not yet shown up. I spent the time, while we waited for it, in visiting the site of the former Institute of Dr. Crossland, where only a few moldering posts now stuck up out of the sand. You could hardly miss the spot, for it was strewn with pearl mussels far and wide. I could well imagine Dr. Crossland, in this most desolate of all wildernesses, methodically and fiercely ransacking mussels— and the government's moneybags. At many places the barbed wire that had once encircled his secret activities was still visible in the sand. It must certainly have been a severe strain on his vitality to endure more than ten years of this neighborhood.

No sign yet of the felucca. As the sky was visibly clouding over again, I began to feel annoyed. At my instigation Mahmud bargained with the fishermen for a boat. I saw him shake his head several times. Finally, he picked up my box, containing all our equipment, and I followed him to the beach. The only boat available was an extremely narrow dugout in which three men at most could sit, one behind the other. Mahmud put the box in it, but there was no sense in that, of course. It might have been possible to paddle out a little way in this contrivance, but the moment I tried to put on my diving gear, we should inevitably have capsized.

I had the box taken out and got into my equipment on the beach. One of the boys standing round was ordered to carry the box and everything else we couldn't take back to the "Rest-Hut." Fins on my feet, spear in my right hand, encased in my respirator, and mask resting on my forehead, I sat down in the middle of the dugout, and it was launched into the water. Mahmud took the rear paddle and the owner the forward one. I still hadn't the least idea how I was going to manage to get in and out. But I didn't care; I was set on examining those pearl banks. If positively necessary, I could always swim back.

We reached deep water, crossed a shallow bank, then deep water again, and another shoal. After going a fairly long way, we lay to and the fisherman, whose features were unusually intelligent, gave me to understand that I could find mussels to my heart's content in the depths below us. As the water looked perfectly dark, I inquired about the depth. He threw out his arms to the width of a yard and a half about thirty times. That meant 135 feet! The man must have thought I was a miracle worker! I hadn't the slightest intention of swimming 135 feet down into the unknown with no rope.

He took us to another spot, where the depth was only seventy-five feet. When I got back to Port Sudan, I discussed with Bill the question of how the fellow could possibly tell that there were particularly rich banks at great depths, for the natives hardly ever go below seventy-five feet. In Bill's opinion the man had probably only guessed at the possibility or was relying on some old tradition. He said a Frenchman had made some investigations there a few years ago, in traditional divers' dress, but had gotten little out of it. The fisherman probably hoped to obtain further information on the subject with me to help him.

The other two leaned over to the left while I climbed over the low edge of the dugout on the right. It was quite an acrobatic performance. As I gradually lowered myself into the water, they had to match my rate of descent as they shifted their weight. It was a wonder the boat didn't capsize after all.

The water was rather turbid. Tiny little jellylike organisms came drifting round me like snowflakes. I swam down. I had no sooner lost sight of the surface than the bottom glimmered up below me. It was flat, sandy, and sloped away a little. When I reached it, I found that it was generously covered with green vegetation and low-growing stumps of coral.

The colonization of this sea bed was quite different from that of the coral reefs, and I came across fish I had never seen before. Large, glassy-looking Salpa passed close by me. On the sand lay strangely hideous sea cucumbers and starfish, and wormlike fish watched me from their holes, retreating when I approached. But, to be frank, I was not very interested in all this. As soon as I had had a good look round in this gloomy twilight in case there were sharks about, I concentrated my attention on pearl mussels only.

It was some time before I found the first one. But after that they seemed to be everywhere. They were not very large and for the most part they stood on end, the separable portions of the shell slightly apart. Many were in bundles of four or five together. The majority grew on corals or rocks, others lay on the sand.

I drew out my knife and swam from one to another, cutting through the muscle and prying the shells apart before they had time to close. I was obsessed with the feverish excitement natural to a seeker of gold or jewels. With trembling hands I felt carefully over the flesh of every single mussel in case it might contain a pearl. A steadily increasing host of fish followed me, squabbling over the dead mussels. If a shark had turned up just then, I should certainly not have noticed it.

After about fifteen minutes of this I calmed down a bit. I began to pay more attention to location and development and gave up imagining that I was absolutely bound to find a splendid pair of earrings in each mussel. I actually did come across little pearls in a few of the mussels, but they were deeply embedded in the shell and therefore worthless. Many shells had diseased growths on them. At last I discovered a fairly large pearl with only a small part of it adhering to the shell.

Just then I saw a shark right in front of me. He was light gray in color, had a pointed snout, was rather plump and without question over nine feet in length. Two large sucking fish were swimming under his belly. I gave a start like that of a boy caught stealing in the pantry and dropped the mussel. The shark, too, gave a start. He whisked round and was gone in an instant, like a phantom.

The sand stirred up in the water, now slowly drifting down, showed the place where he had been a moment ago.

I stayed under water till my oxygen ran out. Now that I had seen one section of the banks, I could easily guess what all the rest looked like. I could tell in advance, from the appearance of certain places, that I should undoubtedly find a mussel there. It was just like looking for mushrooms; the expert soon gets to know under which trees and bushes he had better search most closely.

It was not until I reached the surface that I realized I had gone a good deal deeper than I supposed. I had lost all my bearings in that turbid gloom. I found I was a fairly long way from the boat and swam rapidly toward it. Mahmud and the fisherman seemed to be asleep. When I called to them, they both sat up and paddled over to me.

It was impossible to get aboard in my equipment. I took it off in the water and handed it into the boat piecemeal. Then I vaulted in myself, astern. There was still no sign of our felucca in any direction. Meanwhile, the sky had become completely overcast. No wonder it had been so dark down below.

In our absence a dish of rice had been prepared in the "Rest-Hut"; Omar Effendi had been sleeping in his arm-chair and "Uncle Locusts" had been combing the neighborhood for grasshoppers. We ate together. Sour camel's milk was the drink provided, but this I courteously declined. I wound up the day's proceedings by re-entering the water, from the beach, and there I discovered, among coral beds in quite shallow water, the biggest clam I ever found in the Red Sea. It was quite easy to detach from the corals, and I took the shell back with me to Muhammad Qol. Just as we were driving off, our felucca turned up at last. We directed the fishermen to tell her to return at once.

At the fort, over tea in "Uncle Locusts'" room, I inquired about the small island in the middle of the atoll. Its name was Angarosh, which means "Mother of Sharks." The old fisherman's face did not move a muscle when he heard that I meant to sail there in the morning. But Mahmud surveyed us with a rather peculiar expression. He promised to wake me the moment there was a slight breeze.

233

IN THE SHOAL
OF THE MONSTERS

IN THE SHOAL OF THE MONSTERS

WE DASHED through the tossing waves like a racing craft. There didn't seem to be much sense in what we were doing. Clouds covered the whole sky, rain fell at intervals, and the wind was steadily rising. The waves were so high that when we slid down into their troughs tall masses of water arched over us on every side. But I only had two days left; this one was to be devoted to the "Mother of Sharks" and the next to Mukawwar. We might never get to the shark island, and if we did I might not be able to dive there, but still I didn't want to miss the chance. Mahmud, moreover, with the calm confidence of a weather prophet, predicted that before midday the whole sky would be blue again.

The fisherman who owned the boat had on this occasion brought a little boy with him for company. The two of them cowered timidly, cheek by jowl, beside the mast. No doubt the old fellow had never been out before in such weather. Mahmud, on the other hand, was thoroughly in his element.

As the entire sea was a mass of foam, it was much more difficult than usual to recognize the coral reefs. Mahmud, his turban fluttering, steered past the walls of reef and through narrow channels between them. I forgave him his trespasses at that moment. This native really had guts as well as humor.

And it seemed as though he could not only rule the waves, but the heavens too, for in the far distance a big blue patch was rapidly appearing; and by about half-past eleven the whole sky had been swept clear of cloud. It became a glorious day! The glowing, wildly agitated sea surged beneath us in deepest ultramarine, while the foaming wave crests sparkled like the bubbles in a champagne glass. To our right the broad cliffs of the island of Mukawwar flashed brilliantly in the sun; to our left we could now see for the first time the promontory of Ras Abu Shagara, encircling, like an arm, in a wide arc, the pearl-fishing bay of Dungunab.

The sea raged over a number of small islands, tossing its foaming arms high into the sunny air, as though in the wildest spirits. The coast itself had the appearance of a gray streak, above which towered, from a base of mist, the mighty peaks of the mountain ranges. Muhammad Qol and its fort were no longer visible; the curve of the watery surface of the globe had already hidden them. Stormy petrels were soaring aloft in joyous exuberance, drifting at giddy heights before the wind, and then swooping down again in dives that had the speed of an arrow. Our fisherman and his boy alone took no part in the general exultation of nature. Thoroughly frightened and thinking only of themselves, they crouched by the mast, holding each other tight.

Mahmud rose to his feet excitedly. He gave me the tiller to hold, jumped up on the thwart, and shaded his eyes. He explained to me by signs that we were about to enter the atoll. We should then, he gave me to understand, find ourselves in much smoother water. As we proudly glided up the side of a mountainous wave, we perceived a long line of foam confronting us. We should have to pass through it at some point or other. Behind the line of foam, in the far distance, a slender, vertical streak rose above the horizon. This was apparently a reef signal, and Mahmud steered straight for it.

Where could the entrance of the atoll be? Mahmud, without ceasing to look keenly ahead, rummaged impatiently in his labyrinthine pockets and extracted his little tin of chewing tobacco. He popped a good-sized lump of it into his mouth. Suddenly he let out a yell of triumph and instantly resumed his seat at the tiller.

We passed through that ominous barrier and came, in fact, into considerably smoother water. The vertical streak in front of us increased in height. It was not merely a reef signal, but a tall steel structure which evidently carried an automatic, intermittent beacon. In another half-hour we had reached it. It stood on a longish section of reef, which I assumed to be part of the outer ring. The sea beyond it was raging yards high, but on our side the water was almost entirely smooth.

"Angarosh?" I asked.

"Angarosh! Angarosh!" Mahmud nodded his agreement. Grinning all over his face, he gave me to understand that particularly hideous sharks were to be found in this locality. I was surprised to learn that this place was the "Mother of

239

Sharks." From the map I had supposed the island to be smaller, and I was also unable to convince myself that this was the center of the ring of reefs. The steel scaffolding had obviously only recently been erected. It was 100 or 125 feet high and a concrete path led right across the top of the reef to the wide emplacement. Mahmud moored the boat and I slipped overboard.

The reef wall, like that of the lighthouse at Sanganeb, fell away perpendicularly, but to a much greater depth. I dived down alongside it but could not see where it ended. At the top, where the surf raged, the wall had been hollowed out in places; further down it became completely smooth, with small corals growing outward from it. When they were seen from above, they seemed to be growing upward in the ordinary way from a flat area. The appearance of the fish, too, complemented this curious impression; they didn't swim in the usual way, so that I saw their backs when I looked down, but vertically to the wall, probably to keep me in view with their laterally placed eyes.

Though everything in the submarine world may go on just about the same as before, when a diver enters it in some way or other the alien invasion is everywhere noted and inquisitively appraising eyes inspect the intruder from all directions. Two smallish sharks were swimming up and down the wall but I could not see any larger ones. No doubt this reef was most remarkable and unusual in many ways, but I told myself, just the same, that it couldn't possibly be the "Mother of Sharks."

"Angarosh?" I asked Mahmud again when I came to the surface. He nodded, with visible uneasiness. He assured me eagerly that he had known Angarosh ever since he had been

I threw myself aside only just in time as a pair of mantas, which seemed to have gone absolutely mad in their courtship, tore past me.

With his huge quadrangular mouth gaping widely, the big manta made straight for me. Beneath the belly of nearly every manta swam a large sucking fish which made no use of the suctorial disk on the top of its head. Rather it imitated every movement of the manta with dexterous strokes of its tail.

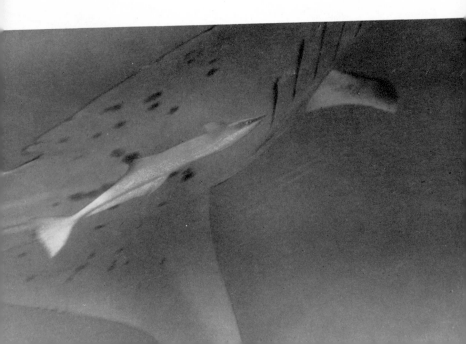

I had difficulty getting a photograph of the pilot fish which re-
sided in the mouths of the biggest mantas. Then I found a manta
that was deformed by nature—his right head lobe was missing.

I stealthily swam up to the right side of the deformed manta and photographed the pilot fish as they swam along at the edge of his huge jaw. Then, to get an even better view of these pilot fish, I made my way above his back, between the swinging flippers, as far as his head, and pointed the camera down over his jaws.

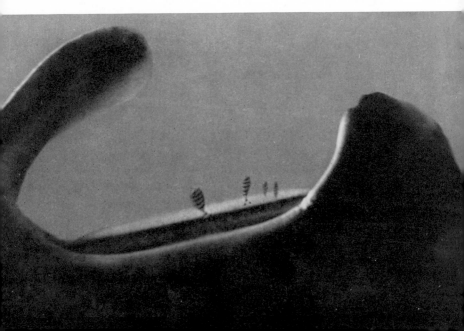

a boy and that there was no other island of the same name. The old fisherman and the boy avoided my glances. They had lighted a charcoal fire aboard, in a ramshackle receptacle, and the smell of brewing coffee filled the air.

There was something wrong here somewhere.

I crawled up to the path, left my fins, mask, harpoon, and camera behind, and walked over to the scaffolding of the reef signal, which I climbed, despite the high wind, by a rope that hung to one side of it. Soon the boat down below began to look small and I could see all over the atoll in all directions. It was exactly as I had thought. We were on the outer ring of the reef and in the center of the atoll, precisely as the map had shown it, lay a small, circular island.

I climbed down at once and gave instructions to leave. I didn't take the slightest notice of Mahmud's protests. I gave him to understand that I had seen through his deception, that I was very annoyed and offended, and that consequently my tip was going to be a very moderate one. All the rascality disappeared from Mahmud's features. He shrugged his shoulders and unmoored the boat.

We entered a rather heavier swell again. As we now had the wind behind us, we soon came in sight of the little island. It was a semicircular heap of rubble with a diameter of at most ninety feet. There was a small pyramid of rock in the middle of it, and it was surrounded by exceptionally high breakers. The only possible moorage would be on the side sheltered from the wind, where the waves, rolling in from right and left, broke over one another, forming an area of turbulence.

God only knows what was the matter with Mahmud: we almost capsized at a point quite close to the island. A wave coming in the opposite direction spun us round, the sail flew over with a rush, a huge breaker caught us from one side, and water came pouring over the bulwark. At the last moment the vessel righted itself and luckily we got into the island's narrow shadow. After strenuous work with the oars we reached the point at the edge of the reef where the two courses of waves met behind the island. As the opposing wave currents never came in at exactly the same time, the craft was continually carried this way and that.

The small charcoal fire aboard had been extinguished as soon as we left the beacon; the old fisherman and the boy were still embracing like a pair of lovers. Mahmud impressed upon me, with great earnestness, that we could only stay here a very short time. Standing up to row, he was adjusting the boat's course to the currents, to prevent her striking on the rocks.

I sprang onto the top of the reef, in shallow water, made the anchor faster than it had been, and dashed across hip-deep water onto the island. It consisted entirely of coral boulders worn to a spherical smoothness, with beautiful red fragments of organ-pipe coral lying between them. I took these back to the boat, together with some other pieces of coral and mussel shell. I was making a collection which included, as well as uninjured specimens, a number that the sea had broken and capriciously re-formed, into the most extraordinary shapes.

Then I put on the mask and dived into the foamy swirls of surf. As soon as my vision cleared, I saw innumerable, glittering, red fish gliding over the projecting domes of green corals. A little further down eighty or a hundred "boobyfish" were swimming. The amazing thing about the view was that I was looking over jutting corals into a bottomless abyss. There was no sign of any reef wall down below. The island seemed to be simply afloat, with fathomless blue water beneath as well as all round it.

The fact of the matter was that the corals which had built up in the zone of the surf had formed a projecting ledge several yards wide, under which I had to dive in order to see the perpendicular wall beneath. On this side the isle resembled a tower rising out of the depths like the stem of a mushroom. It was conceivable that this type of structure had originated spontaneously in a hump of the sea bed. The reason it had not assumed the form of a pyramid but had grown up with vertical edges might be that the marginal corals had the stronger growth and thus came to compose a projecting ledge. If they grew too luxuriantly and dried off, the ledge would crumble and a vertical wall would take its place.

I had reached this point in my reflections when an obscure impulse caused me to turn round. Behind me a giant of a shark, at least twelve feet long, had appeared. He was gliding slowly through the water, like a gleaming projectile, and keeping a watchful eye on me. I quickly focused the camera and photographed him. Then I made a dash for the surface, broke through its cover of foam, took in a rapid breath of air, turned, and made another rush downward.

I was not destined, however, to take a second photograph. The shark had changed his position in my absence and now charged me at full speed. It was obvious, too, that he was not taking this action, as smaller sharks often do, out of sheer curiosity or high spirits, meaning to turn back of his own accord a short distance away. He was coming with the unmistakable intention of attacking me; his tail thrashed the water at ever increasing speed.

The whole of his great body charged me in a single composite rush, the sickle-shaped jaws conspicuous in the van. I swam to meet him, but at once became aware that this particular brute was not to be frightened in that way. There was only one thing that could help me now. Uttering a shrill scream, I puffed against the water.

A surging wave hurled me backward. Despite the speed of his onrush, the shark had spun round just before reaching me and dashed, just like the sharks in the Caribbean, with a terrified beating of his fins, for the depths. But a moment later he had turned back and was rising to the attack again. As I had not enough breath left to give a second yell and it was, moreover, very doubtful whether that would be any use now, my only chance was a precipitate retreat.

By making a supreme effort I managed to cover the few yards between me and the boat and half-heaved myself and half-bounded over its side. Mahmud seized my floundering legs and hauled them aboard. I landed, head first, straight into the charcoal bucket. Then came the sound of rushing waters on the surface and the shark thumped against the boat.

"*Miskois! Miskois!*" Mahmud commented, shaking his head, indicating the shark was bad—wickedly dangerous. Then he seized the oar and thrust it into the water with the same determination he had shown when he had resisted the gorgeously clad Arab in Port Sudan.

The shark dived under the boat and away. He was obviously furious that the tasty morsel had escaped him. I made no protest when the old fisherman, without any orders from me, cast off. The boy hoisted the sail and we began to move. I watched, with a rapidly swelling bruise on my forehead, the "Mother of Sharks" disappearing into the distance behind us.

That there was no wholly reliable defense against the "tigers of the sea" I had known ever since the expedition to Greece, where yelling and screaming had not once been effective. It had worked again on this occasion, though. A certain risk is indissolubly bound up with this method of marine investigation and probably always will be. The chemical expedients developed by the American Navy to protect aviators shot down into the sea would certainly be of no avail against sharks attacking with such rapidity and determination; and even if special poisonous, explosive, or rocket weapons could be constructed, which would kill sharks, the result would merely be, in my experience, to fall out of the frying pan into the fire; for a dying shark, as it thrashed about in the water, would inevitably, in a matter of seconds, attract others to the spot, which would be even more ferocious.

It had taken five hours to sail to the atoll; it took us another five to sail back. Twilight had already set in and Muhammad Qol was already in sight when we passed a place where numerous pointed wave crests flickered, like flames, over the surface of the sea. On closer observation I perceived that they were not waves, but small, pointed fins. No less than forty mantas had assembled there—an enormous shoal of them!

I jumped overboard and saw, at a distance, two big white bellies confronting each other. But it was already too late. It was far too dark now to photograph and take observations under water. As I climbed back into the boat, Mahmud consoled me with his characteristic weather prophet's assurance: I need not worry, the mantas would be sure to be still there the following day, I could take his word for it.

I tossed sleeplessly in my bed that night. If the mantas really were still there in the morning, I shouldn't hesitate a moment to dive in among them. What could they be up to? Was it their matingtime, or what? I had a vision of myself gliding through a purple firmament among a lot of piebald devils who were dancing round me and trying to butt me with their horns. I heard them uttering the most ghastly shrieks and wails—then I awoke. It was the muezzin, calling the faithful to their first prayers. It was still dark outside, probably four or five in the morning.

I couldn't get to sleep again after that. Day gradually dawned outside the square frame of the window. The sky was heavily overcast. When I got up, I could see that the sea was lying like a great flat lump of lead, unruffled by the slightest ripple. A fisherman was cleaning his dugout; a few women were stirring in the desert; the village was waking up. I lay down again and slept like the dead. At nine o'clock Mahmud woke me; soon after, we started.

We beached our craft on a sandbank in the neighborhood of the place where I had seen the mantas. It was Mahmud's opinion that this was the best spot to catch sight of them if they showed up again. While he and the little boy kindled a fire, I wandered about the islet, kept a good lookout, and collected some pretty mussel shells.

In the middle of the island, which was covered with undergrowth, I found a large and perfectly new balloon tire, evidently dropped there from an aircraft. Then I came to a projecting tongue of sand, where pyramid crabs had erected a city of pyramids. They were working away with great industry at these towers; I wondered why. Why did they arrange the sand, dug up from their dens, into layers to form a pyramid; and why did they shape its spire with particular attention? There were no eggs beneath the pyramids, and they were no use as watchtowers to guard against the dangerous water birds. Nor did they serve to throw any shadow across the lair, nor again could it be assumed that the crabs were merely indulging in a pointless amusement.

For fun, I chased one of them which had gotten rather far away from its base; it ran off in a zigzag course, finding its lair with amazing accuracy. Perhaps that was the point of those towers! When the creatures were out looking for food and were surprised by birds, the towers might be useful landmarks to enable them to find their holes.

I began to get impatient. Perhaps this was only another of Mahmud's diversionary maneuvers and the mantas had gone elsewhere. Perhaps he was afraid that I would make him and the fisherman row backward and forward across the sea. On the other hand, the place lay at a certain elevation and really gave a good view over the sea in all directions. Just where had those mantas gone to? Mahmud had indicated to me that we could expect them about midday. That might be so, but it also might be just a trick.

I found a cozy coffee party going on beside the little fire. I was obliged to sit down and accept one of those tiny bowls, without a handle, which cost two piasters each in Port Sudan and were a permanent feature of every fishing vessel's equipment. Mahmud, while he served me with sticky toasted dates, had his right foot stuck out in front of him. He had fastened the end of a fishline to his big toe, and it was trailing in the shallow water. I didn't notice it until something suddenly gave his toe a tug.

He followed the direction of the pull, hopping on one leg. Then he picked up the line and a large fish began to thrash about in the shallows. Must be a ray! I thought. Mahmud dragged and hauled for all he was worth—then he tumbled over backward and the line went slack again.

I had the mask close beside me; with great bounds I dashed into the water. The course taken by the retreating fish was clearly indicated by the stirred up sand. But suddenly, in water six feet deep, the trail ended.

Where on earth had the creature disappeared? I took a closer look at the sandy bottom; then I spotted two eyes, barely visible as they peeped up through the sand. I could now make out the shape of the fish, a slightly arched outline. With a dexterous movement, it had buried itself. It was a halavi, a fiddle-shaped fish that is a queer sort of link between a shark and a skate.

I thought of fetching my harpoon, then a better idea occurred to me. I cautiously edged closer to the spot where the rather long tail could just be distinguished, owing to the presence of three fins which showed inconspicuously above the sand. With a swift movement I grabbed for, and caught, the tail! The halavi struggled and struck out in all directions, but I hung on tight. I had to be careful, however, that the little devil didn't bite me. A gelatinous, transparent, shovel-shaped nose stood out from his head and he was brandishing it about with great vigor. First he pulled me down and then I pulled him up. Finally I mastered his struggling and hauled him into shallow water, where an overjoyed Mahmud grasped him.

There was still no sign of the mantas. For some time, at a rather distant spot, birds had been fluttering about over the water. I realized then that I had seen the same kind of birds the day before, over the place where the mantas had been. I immediately had the boat cleared for action and we rowed in that direction.

Mahmud and the fisherman both agreed that in the other direction—which we could sail to, instead of rowing—there would be a great many more mantas. But I wasn't taken in by that trick. Both bent, sighing, to the oars and began to sing African laments. It sounded like a litany. Mahmud would gasp out a stanza, in a voice which continually broke, and the other two, for the boy chimed in with the old man, would answer with the refrain. As we were rowing right in the teeth of the wind, our progress was agonizingly slow. Nevertheless we went faster than we could have gone with the sail, for these keel-less boats are so helpless before the wind that they are driven back almost to the same place from which they start.

Our voyage inched along for more than an hour before we reached "manta ground." The whole sea seemed to be on the boil there. The screams of the flocks of birds warned us that we were very far from being welcome. Everywhere small fish were leaping from the surface and being seized and swallowed by the birds. And everywhere below the surface gigantic jaws were sweeping along and swallowing everything in their path.

I took several photographs from the boat, then I dropped overboard. At first I could only see innumerable fish rushing to and fro in excited shoals. They were being chased not only by the mantas and the birds but also by mackerel and long fish that had a silvery glitter. Then the wall of fish before me parted and a big manta made straight for me.

He didn't seem to see me at all. He came fluttering along, as though in a blissful trance. I took several photographs, focusing nearer and nearer—I took one of the square jaws —but the giant continued to swim calmly on. He swam on right over me, his eyes fixed and glassy. He actually touched me, and at the same instant spun round, his flukes whipping, and gave me a terrific thump on the back. I thought my spine had broken in two. Though the jaws of these creatures might not be dangerous—for I had just carefully observed them and there was only one sparse row of teeth along the lower mandible—their movements in fright were certainly so. A brief loss of consciousness would have finished me. The water I was swimming in was abysmally deep.

Hanging onto the side of the boat, I regained my self-possession. Several mantas were now sweeping along very close to the boat, and I also saw two a long way down, gliding past with their powerful strokes. I had used up all my film while I had been swimming about among the creatures, and now I had to put a new supply in the camera.

The mantas were mostly brown; some were pitch-black; one had a queer, discolored patch on the back. They swam alone, in pairs, or in whole families of three or four at a time, and greedily dredged up the fish and sea snails that glided along in the water. The disproportion between their terrific jaws and the diminutive prey they used them for was as grotesque as that between the trunk of an elephant and the peanut one tosses him. Like fantastic, monstrous birds they swung along through the water with regular upward and downward beats of their flippers, the bizarre lobes attached to their heads flapping, as they stretched them sideways and then drew them together in front of the jaws to capture their prey.

In the case of two specimens, which I could distinguish by their external peculiarities, I clearly perceived that they could recognize me after the third or fourth encounter. In the case of fish—though the latter stand higher on the ladder of evolution—I had never noticed such a thing. I found it interesting to observe that the mental faculties of these rays, and of most sharks, seem to exceed, in this respect, those of fish.

While remaining ceaselessly on the watch, in order to evade further disagreeable encounters, I did my best to get in among the creatures and photograph the big sucking fish that were swimming beneath nearly every one of the smooth, white bellies.

I noted with interest that these sucking fish made no use at all of the suctorial disk placed on top of their heads. They imitated every movement of the manta with dexterous strokes of their tails and always kept in the same position. When a manta spun round in a fright and made off, they, too, swam faster than before and though at first they might be left a little behind, they soon overhauled the manta; it looked as though they were attached to his belly by a piece of elastic. They probably only sucked at night, when at rest. By day they had to join in the chase and snap up anything the manta let fall under its belly.

I threw myself aside only just in time as a pair that seemed to have gone absolutely mad tore past me. By now

I had a pretty good idea of what went on during the mating season in so large a shoal as this. Even the brief performance of which I was a witness had so furious a character that the two creatures simply ran down everything that got in their way.

I returned to the boat, which followed the shoal all the time, put in a new film, and was back in the water in a trice. The phenomena I was observing, though there was no mistake about them, were so fantastic that I almost came to believe that I was fast asleep and dreaming. I had never felt so physically fit as I did just then. I had absolutely no fear of anything and the common exultation of all these surging bodies communicated itself to me, by a kind of irradiation, as if I were myself a member of the shoal. It was a feverish and giddy intoxication such as I had never known in my life before. I was barely conscious of my brief dashes to the surface for air.

I discovered, in the jaws of the biggest manta, some little fish that were darting about. I had no difficulty in identifying these, from their transverse stripes, as pilot fish, the very creatures that are said to guide the shark to his prey. In order to keep them under observation, I followed the giant for a time and tried to get him used to me, so that he would let me come nearer to his gaping jaws. Twice he gave a start of fright, but on each occasion I managed quickly to safeguard my head in time. I did it by wrapping myself up into a ball, with my head and camera in the middle of it.

According to my observations, the pilot fish behaved like lodgers; they had first-rate protection, in the jaws, from all dangers and certainly they didn't lack food. Their unconcern somewhat reminded me of that of the aristocrats imprisoned during the French Revolution, who continued to dance their gavottes and stage their pastoral plays in the jail itself, as they awaited execution. The comparison, to be sure, is not too close, for the fishlets did not have to force themselves, in the slightest degree, to be merry. For some mysterious reason the manta put up with them and did not gobble them up—very much in the same way as jellyfish treat their guider fish, and giant sea anemones, their pomacentrids. The solution of the mystery is no doubt the same in the case of "the devil." Probably the pilot fish clean the manta's jaws, especially the lower row of teeth, among which, I learned later, small parasitic crayfish settle. The pilot fish scrub the manta's jaws and teeth—such is the nature of the rent they have to pay for their comfortable quarters.

Unfortunately it was quite impossible to get near enough to these pilot fish to photograph them. For one thing the manta would not allow it, and for another the fish immediately retreated deeper into the shadow of their protector's jaws when I approached. Moreover, the broad lobes to right and left were in the way and made it impossible to get a view of the interior. I tried coming up from below, but this made the manta nervous and he swam so fast that I could barely keep up with him. All I got for my pains were a few more thumps.

Then I found another manta, deformed by nature in a manner that suited me. His right head-lobe was missing, so that I could see into his jaws from that side. I slyly glided up from that direction and managed to take a photograph under his very eye without being observed. Later, when he was swimming in a depth of fifteen feet, I made my way along his back, between the swinging flippers, as far as his head

MANTA

and pointed the camera down over his upper jaw. On this occasion, too, I was not noticed by the pilot fish till I had taken the photograph. Then the manta himself noticed me . . . I rolled myself into a ball and let the resulting thunderstorm pass harmlessly away from me.

For my final effort I put in a color film and repeated the photographs already taken. Then I fetched the movie camera and shot a long sequence showing the jaws of a manta coming right at the camera. I had by this time spent two hours among the mantas, which now gradually began to disperse.

One of the creatures with a misshapen tumor on its head behaved in rather an extraordinary manner. It shook itself as though it were trying to get rid of something and made an attempt to put me to flight by swimming straight at me.

I thought I would have a try at killing this monster, with a view to examining it later. If I tied the barb of the harpoon to the boat with a fairly long rope and then drove the harpoon through the manta's flipper, so that his escape would be impeded on one side, that might do the trick.

I returned to the boat at once and twisted the whole of my reserve stock of wire into a long end piece. I collected all the lines I had and made them, together with the anchor rope, into a strong noose. If my plan succeeded, I should be able to take the skin back with me to a museum. The creature could not have weighed less than twelve hundred pounds, but just then nothing seemed impossible to me.

I did not have to swim around the boat very long before I saw that black fellow again. He bobbed up a little to my right. I followed him up and sent the harpoon whizzing diagonally through one of his flippers. Next moment the iron shaft had been bent into a right angle and the rope ran out at terrific speed. From the surface I saw the boat suddenly swing round and make off, with the rope over its bow. Mahmud, the old fisherman, and the boy were yelling and gesticulating. It looked as though the boat had suddenly been fitted with an engine.

Then the boat stopped and began to turn. It was clear that the manta was trying to make a perpendicular dive. Mahmud rushed to seize the rope and hoist it in. The main weight of the vessel being forward and the ray pulling backward, the bow sank deep under water and the stern rose. And as the manta was obviously swimming in a circle, with incessant beating of its flippers, the boat also spun round and round, tilting up and down as it went.

I swam as fast as I could in the direction of the craft, intending to swarm down the anchor rope with my knife. But I was not destined to get as far as that. I caught sight of a shark that was also making at full speed for the boat. As it shot past me, I saw the manta, almost at the same moment, leap high in the air quite close to the boat. Mahmud tried to grab the rope, but it was torn out of his hand; with a jerk and a sharp report it broke in two.

"Big shark!" beamed Mahmud, as I climbed into the boat.

"Big baksheesh!" I retorted, in the best of humors. Indeed the rascally Mahmud would get a substantial tip! His misdemeanors were few when weighed against his delightfully roguish companionship and his dependability in a crisis.

I felt no trace yet of the exhaustion that was bound to ensue. I had been swimming among the mantas for more than two hours and had photographed everything that could be photographed. No wonder I was pleased. The pictures would undoubtedly make a new expedition a certainty.

As I lay back on the deck and let Mahmud and the old fisherman pilot the felucca back to Muhammad Qol, once again I envisioned my longed-for research vessel, with swelling sails, bearing down in the offing.

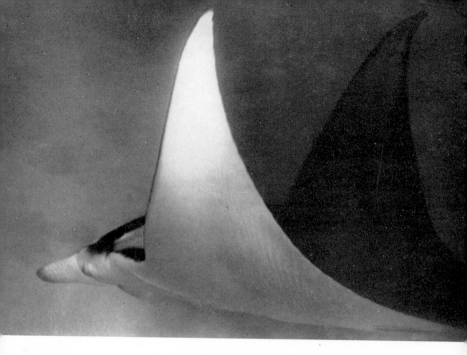

Like fantastic monstrous birds the mantas swung through the water with regular upward and downward beats of their flippers, the grotesque lobes attached to their heads flapping as they stretched them sideways and then drew them together in front of the jaws to capture their prey.

I watched pyramid crabs build spired heaps of sand from the residue dug up from their lairs.

A young hammerhead shark with its queerly shaped head is another Red Sea creature.

The only signs that remained of Dr. Crossland's former Institute were posts and pearl-mussel shells.

Every morning this old beggar showed me the hideous skin disease that affected his feet and accepted the coin I gave him without the slightest word of thanks.

Christmastime on an African desert! And the Fuzzy-Wuzzies brought me a camel to ride. The camel had to get used to the smell of his new rider, and I had to get used to the curious bumpy gait.

THE LAST DAY

THE LAST DAY

THE VALET had found out that I was leaving in the morning and presented himself for his modest remuneration. The old fisherman also called for his wages and grinned for the first time when he was given considerably more than he asked for. "Uncle Locusts" had said good-by to me earlier in the day. He had left at noon. Omar Effendi, to whom Mahmud had shown the harpoon twisted to a right angle, was even more friendly than he had been before. Although we could not exchange a single word with each other, we were now on excellent terms. He gave me to understand that he intended to accompany me in the truck tomorrow as far as the Fuzzy village at the halfway point.

I went to bed early and slept like a log. Next morning I was told that our truck had arrived in good time, actually during the night. While I packed, I tried hard to realize that it was Christmastime. At home there would be snow and ice and gaily decorated Christmas trees in warm living rooms; here the heat of the new day was aglare all round the fort. Down below, between the door and the truck, a guard of honor composed of local beggars was lining up.

The chief of them was an old man with a hideous skin disease on his feet. He had lain in wait for me every morning at the entrance to the fort and had approached me on each occasion with the same imperiously challenging gesture. He would then pocket, without the slightest smattering of a word of thanks, the small coin I handed him. It was not a request he had made, but a demand, the imposition of which appeared to be authorized in his case by an inner conviction of his rights. His example was followed, that day, by all the other beggars. As I came out of the fort, still dispensing a few more tips, the silent ranks closed in peremptorily upon me.

Fortunately I had enough coins on me to satisfy them all. I had also provided myself with some small pieces of money for the children, over which they instantly began to quarrel at the tops of their voices. For the first time, some young women and girls showed themselves at the doors of the huts. They had all gotten to know me well by peeping through the chinks of the boarding and also by hearsay, and now they felt they must show themselves too, before I drove away.

We took the same road we had come by. At a certain spot, where we saw three gazelles, Omar Effendi called a halt. He had an old-fashioned shotgun with him and let fly a load of shot at one of the creatures, which was regarding us with a trustful expression. It was pitiful to see the gazelle, with the small shot in its body, running away and then collapsing. Fortunately the rest kept out of range of the gun.

It turned out that the gazelle had been shot in my special

honor. As soon as we had gone halfway and arrived at the lonely settlement of Fuzzies, Omar Effendi made us stop and signed to me to get out. Although it was really my intention to be back again in Port Sudan before dark, I couldn't very well decline this hospitable offering, which was also made for the benefit of the driver and Mahmud. A wooden camp bed was dragged out of one of the huts and set up in the shadow of the wall of a house; I was invited to make myself comfortable on it. Meanwhile a fire was lighted and the flesh of the gazelle was roasted. In a circle before my couch a ring of magnificent looking Fuzzies sat facing me. Then an older, even more dignified Fuzzy presented himself, saluted me in friendly fashion, and sat down in an armchair which had been placed beside the couch. This, Mahmud explained to me, was the *Omda*.

Everyone drank coffee and ate pieces of the meat, which had been roasted on hot stones, and I was myself obliged, whether I liked it or not, to devour, as a special tidbit, the whole of the roast liver. Mahmud was the star of the mealtime conversation. He gave an account of our exploits, in which, so far as I could understand from his gestures, he declared that he himself had taken part, accompanying all my descents and observations. The audience hung upon his story with expressions of incredulous amazement. They often burst out laughing, while the *Omda* shook his head, nodding at me amicably.

I had to confess to myself that I felt rather more at my ease in this gathering and these less than luxurious surroundings than I had on previous Christmas holidays. Somehow or other the gloriously clear outline of the rocky landscape and the unearthly purity of the radiant sky gave me a sense of contentment and satisfaction such as I had hardly ever known in the bustle of the metropolis. From the shadows of an open door I saw a dark pair of eyes directed unwinkingly upon me. It was the same young girl I had seen at the fountain.

When the meal at last came to an end and we had all formally belched and expressed our appreciation of the entertainment, the *Omda,* just as I was getting up, inquired of me, the driver translating for him, whether I would care to stay with him as his guest for a few days. Unluckily, it was out of the question. Bill was expecting me and would probably send a car to look for me if I didn't turn up. But I was glad to accept Omar Effendi's invitation, when some camels were led up, to go for a little ride with him.

At first it was a bit bumpy; then I got used to the curious gait. We rode across one of the high mounds of dead rock and then over a plain which led some distance into the hills. The ride lasted forty minutes and I then took leave of Omar Effendi and the *Omda.* The door of that hut was shut now. As we drove on, I could not help thinking how little all that we call civilization would increase the happiness of these people.

Just before we got to Port Sudan, when it was already dark, the driver took a "short cut" and we got lost in the desert. We had to shovel sand, in the pitch-darkness, to get the truck out of a dune. That happened over and over again. Finally we found a hard surface under our wheels and reached Port Sudan by driving hell for leather over bush and steppe alike.

Bill was not at home; he turned up while I was having

a bath. There was not much time for talking, for we had two parties to attend before the ball at the club. The next day, a Sunday, the English community would assemble at midday for a turkey dinner, and that evening a gala supper would be served at the Red Sea Hotel.

At the ball two masters from the school at Khartoum were present, as well as a lively young geography mistress. While I was dancing with her, she told me she was studying old chronicles in the Government Library. She mentioned that she had read about a Russian ship which had sunk sixty years ago halfway from Port Sudan to Suakin.

"Whereabouts is the wreck?" I asked.

"You'd like to see it?"

"I might."

"Well, I'll only tell you where it is if you promise to take me with you."

"All right, I promise."

If the ship had really been under water for so long, it would certainly afford most interesting points of comparison with the *Umbrea*. It should be possible, aboard her, to observe the formation and progressive development of a new community of living beings under the same sort of conditions. After the first corals, acting as pacemakers, had encrusted the ironwork, the rest would be bound to follow in a certain order.

When Mahmud presented himself the following morning, I asked Bill to try and get some information from him about the ship. Mahmud answered at once that he knew all about her; she lay, he said, in about ninety feet of water and was completely smashed up. We could drive by truck along the Suakin Road as far as a certain fishing village and there hire a felucca. As my aircraft did not leave for another two days, I instructed Mahmud to order a vehicle for the following day. Then I called up the geography mistress and told her we should be starting early the next morning.

I confirmed the booking of my reserved seat in the plane, and packed up my collections in a box to be sent by the next vessel that left for Europe. In the afternoon I drove with Bill to Flamingo Bay, the harbor at Port Sudan set apart for sailing craft. Mussels were being loaded there at the time and the whole air stank. The thirty or forty sambuks lying about in the shallow muddy bay at all angles had a picturesque but also a very squalid appearance. The owner of the best of the assortment was waiting for us; it was the same stout Arab whom Mahmud had swindled out of his money. He was very gorgeously clad on this occasion also, in violent contrast to the dirty, poverty-stricken creatures who rowed us out to two of his ships.

These sambuks were nothing more than prettily painted, perfectly hollow hulls, with small decks fore and aft, on which two slanting masts were rigged. The vessels were all thick with dirt and swarming with vermin. But the stout man informed us that if I made up my mind to take one of them, it would be cleaned up and fitted with a deck by the time I returned, with assistants, from Vienna. The smaller of the two craft needed a crew of twelve, the larger one of from eighteen to twenty-four. The charges he quoted were altogether disproportionate to what he offered, but the man knew perfectly well that there was not a single motor-boat I could hire on the whole coast and that his sailing vessels were all we had to choose from. I chose the smaller.

The childlike old fellow in the center was said to have been one of the crew of the Russian ship sunk sixty years ago.

Under the Red Sea the ship had now, for the most part, turned into a coral reef.

How fast do coral formations build up? Here at the left is the rail of the *Umbrea*, sunk only nine years before.....

And here is the rail of the Russian ship sunk sixty years ago. Fifty years' time can alter the appearance of a sunken vessel immensely!

The deck of the former Russian ship was over-grown with coral and re-sembled a thickly plant-ed flower bed.

Amidst all this beauty a ferocious-looking spiny-rayed perch guarded the interior of the Russian vessel.

Five times a day the Mohammedan bows his head toward Mecca.
Amid inhospitable surroundings he submits resignedly to his fate.

When we got back to the house, we found the garden swarming with workmen who were hanging Chinese lanterns on the bushes and had dragged all the armchairs and carpets out into the open. I learned from Bill that the big garden party which he had to give every year at Christmastime, as senior official of the town, would take place that evening, after the annual supper. In the dining room several women were busy with mountainous piles of sandwiches and caterers were constantly coming and going with something or other.

I drove to the Shell Works to get my oxygen cylinders filled again, for the last time.

"So you're leaving us?" the director inquired when I arrived. "When you came to see us the first time, I would have bet anything something would go wrong with that plan of yours."

"You'd have lost," I said. "We'll be on the job again tomorrow."

That evening, for the last time, I resignedly donned my evening clothes. The first guests were already streaming into the park and Bill and I had to fulfill our duties as hosts.

The party was a great success. All round the lawn open fires had been lighted, for it was winter even here and the nights were only lukewarm. Bill made a speech which was received with enthusiastic applause, while groups of people stood and sat about everywhere, enjoying relays of drinks and sandwiches. Achmed had no less than eight boys under his command, ceaselessly circulating among the guests as they served the refreshments. I danced with the wife of the champion swimmer. She was completely mollified again and even asked me to show her my collection of mussels. When the dance music stopped, we heard monotonous singing and wailing in the distance. The Feast of the Prophet had begun. The faithful were collecting on the outskirts of the town and commencing their rituals.

We made an early start next morning. The young geography mistress had brought the botany master with her and introduced him to me as her husband. After a drive of an hour and a half in the direction of Suakin we pulled up in the open road and walked over to the sea. Extensive mangrove swamps bordered the beach. The aspect of the desert had changed a great deal owing to the rains. Grass was growing everywhere and herds of camels were browsing.

We had to wade for some distance through deep mud before we came to the place where our hired boat was waiting for us. Great herons winged past us, gliding in slow motion. Using sticks to push our way through the mud, we followed the winding banks of a mangrove-edged lagoon till we reached its outlet to the sea, where a felucca was lying ready. It was even smaller and more worm-eaten than the one at Muhammad Qol.

A few fishermen had built extremely primitive dwellings for themselves among the bushes. Mahmud drew our attention to an amiably smiling, somewhat foolish-looking old fellow, whom he alleged to be the last survivor of the former shipwreck. The botany master, who understood a little Arabic, put a few questions to him on the subject. But there was nothing to be gotten out of the old chap but silly grins and amiable nods. Mahmud gallantly offered our lady companion his hand and helped her aboard the felucca.

On this occasion, too, there was plenty of wind. As soon

as we had left the shallow reefs behind us, we encountered a considerable swell. Five minutes later the botany master, Mr. Brooks, had turned pale. I saw that he was fighting a plucky but hopeless battle against seasickness. I felt sorry for him, for we couldn't possibly turn back now on his account. But he bore his lot, uncomplaining, and did not ask to be returned to shore.

After a voyage of an hour and a half we reached our destination. The vessel had obviously been tossed onto the reef by a southerly gale; as the wind was now in the north, she was lying, so far as we were concerned, in sheltered waters. Mahmud made fast to a short piece of iron that stuck out a few inches above water of moderate depth. I at once verified by peering under water that we were over the ship's bow, about the only iron part of the vessel that could still be recognized in detail, the rest of the wreck having been completely broken up by gales. It had fallen to pieces and corals had grown all over it; it had thus become a coral reef, above which only a few girders and fragments of iron plating were visible.

As clouds were covering the sun, submarine visibility was not very good. A dark wall was rising above the horizon and coming nearer. The botany master by now was not feeling a bit well, and prudence and charity seemed to point to a hasty return to shore. But an inner voice simultaneously informed me that I really couldn't let my final effort end in this way. I had a presentiment that there was still something left to be done. Accordingly, I begged to be excused for the moment, said I should not be long, donned my equipment, and slid overboard. I swam down, right across the murky heap of ruins that had once been a ship.

As the depth increased, the ruins became more and more massive. In one place I saw a thickly overgrown ladder, in another the rounded surface of an ancient boiler; elsewhere however, the vessel had been so utterly broken up that here, too, it was impossible to distinguish between superstructure and substructure.

You could get between the plates into the former interior compartments; I saw a big moray eel there, coiling out of one black cavity into another. There were a great many fish, also, some swimming up and down among the ruins, others lying in wait in the various apertures. Suddenly I found I could see right ahead, where the afterpart of the ship still lay intact, looking like an indistinct drawing through the veil of sunless waters, as it slanted down into the depths.

I was looking at the former deck. The mast had broken off and all the wooden fittings had long since rotted away. The iron girders were still visible, running lengthwise and across the hull; they were covered a yard thick with luxuriant growths of coral. A rail, still partially intact, enclosed the area. Madrepora corals had formed a number of tabular structures of circular shape, with diameters of over six feet, which rose above the center of the former deck. All the ironwork looked as if it were covered with millions of tiny blossoms. I had never seen so many different kinds of corals growing together in so small a space. Though it was very dark, I thought I might be able to take some photographs at full exposure. I raised the camera; then two things happened at once.

The first one was that the camera wouldn't work. Secondly, when I shook it, there was a crack and the stopper of the line from the oxygen cylinder to the respirator began to emit oxygen in a surging stream of bubbles. I made one frantic dash upward to the boat.

Meanwhile it had grown still darker and the black wall on the horizon had come noticeably nearer. Mahmud declared emphatically that there was a storm coming up. I didn't say much in reply, but climbed aboard and unscrewed the stopper from the rest of my gear. I still meant to photograph what I had seen down below and wasn't going to be put off. The storm would just have to wait till I had finished.

Mrs. Brooks watched with deep concern as I repaired the stopper. Then I opened the camera. Water had gotten into it, but only a little and the one film I had used was not spoiled. As I couldn't unwind it backward, I had to take it off in the changing bag and turn it back with my fingers. I asked Mrs. Brooks to lend me her big towel and spread it over my head to keep off splashes. Thus sheltered, I took the camera to pieces and tried to dry the mechanism with the corner of my handkerchief. But the spool still stuck.

My next step was to dismantle the thing. I didn't care a hang what I did to it now, I should probably never use it after tomorrow anyhow. Beyond the shelter of the towel, at which the wind was now tugging, an unearthly human silence reigned. Only at rare intervals did Mrs. Brooks and her husband exchange a whisper; I am sure they both thought I had gone quite mad.

I dried all the wheels and springs and reassembled the apparatus in grim silence. The shutter still didn't work. One of the slides stuck every time. I rattled the shutter fifty, a hundred times, then I got to the point of realizing the senselessness of my behavior. I also became conscious of the steadily growing resentment of the rest of the occupants of the boat. So I decided to give in, rattled the shutter just once more—and the slide, for the first time, dropped into place.

I rattled the thing another hundred times and it worked on almost every occasion. I rapidly put in a high-sensitivity film and fitted the camera into its case again. I had to tackle one last difficulty: water had gotten into the inner side of the glass of the lens, and I had no soap with me to rub it off to prevent the glass from becoming dimmed under water.

"Mahmud! Snuff!" I called out, as I emerged from my lair.

Mahmud looked at me as if there were no doubt now that I was completely demented. Speechless, he handed me his tin of chewing tobacco. I took a pinch of it and rubbed it against the inside of the lens. The tobacco was, to be sure, greasier and softer than soap; but it would serve the purpose just the same.

The wind was rising higher now. While I strapped on my gear, I assured the others that we would be off in ten minutes. Then I slipped overboard again.

I swam straight down to the deck, where I took all the photographs I needed for comparative purposes and got as far as the rear end of the ship, which was clear of the rock. I found its iron plating thickly encrusted with mussels as big as my fist. I should have had to use a hammer and chisel in order to read the vessel's name. Then I set my teeth and swam between two girders into the interior.

A big spiny-rayed perch received me and escorted me over the two decks of the hull. Four months later, when I revisited the spot in delightful weather, he was there again to welcome me. He considered himself the master of the vessel and showed his teeth irritably when I took his portrait.

I made a few more rapid close-ups and dashed back to the surface.

Mahmud cast off and we sailed away. We crossed mountains and valleys of waves. Once I heard Mahmud call upon Allah and all good spirits; there was a crash, but we got past a reef without serious damage. As we couldn't reef the sail we had to let it fly loose; it fluttered, crackled with loud reports, and threatened to tear itself to shreds at any moment. It was a race against time, a gamble of minutes. The black wall of cloud followed us like a menacing phantom. On the horizon there was already no line of division between the rain and the sea. With ominous crashings and splinterings we came floundering, at last, in among the shallow reefs. Swiftly, I seized the camera and helped Mrs. Brooks ashore; Mahmud assisted her husband, now almost prostrate with seasickness; then we salvaged the boat and the rest of our equipment. We had only just gotten across the lagoon when the rain began to fall in great white sheets and the wind howled through the mangroves. That evening we all had whiskies together and laughed over our earlier anxieties.

I had ordered a farewell supper for Bill and myself at the Ramona. The rain had stopped again and we were able to eat at one of the tables set out on the pavement. Between us we calculated that I had arrived in Port Sudan thirty-seven days before. Bill did not think I had been there so long, but I felt as though several months had elapsed.

The white figures passing in the street stood out picturesquely against the dark background of the park. In the distance the rhythmical cries of the faithful resounded; from a nearby café came the squeaking of an Arab phonograph record. The old chemist was sitting at a neighboring table and greeted us in dumb show. Later on the man without arms came and begged at the tables. As soon as he saw me, he immediately squatted down on the ground and extracted his greasy pack of cards from his pocket with his toes. Two days later I should be back in Vienna! I knew by this time that I was going to be homesick for Port Sudan.

Next morning Bill drove me to the airfield, where Mahmud, whom I had substantially rewarded, came to see me off, accompanied by his four children. Nothing would serve but that I should also hand out baksheesh to every child in turn. On my return, he declared, I could place every reliance upon him. By that time he would have a sambuk of his own and would be ready for anything. At the Customs we had trouble again because no one knew I was leaving that day, and there was not enough spare cash available to pay me back my deposit on the cameras. Bill happened to have in his wallet the sum required and paid it over on behalf of the Customs. Then we said good-by to each other.

"In three months' time, then?" Bill said, as we shook hands.

"Yes. In three months' time. By the middle of April at the latest."

He announced that he would postpone his leave till July. I thanked him once again for his hospitality, climbed aboard, and the plane took off. I looked back to see Bill waving his hand and all four of Mahmud's children flourishing their handkerchiefs.

We mounted in a great circle over the chessboard pattern of the town and the white lines that marked the coral reefs in the sea. As we flew along the coast I could also see the islands of Mukawwar and Mayetib and tried to make out the atoll and the islet of Angarosh. Then I lay back in my seat and closed my eyes. An episode in my life, complete in itself, had come to an end. It was an adventure such as I would never, perhaps, enjoy to the same extent again.

GLOSSARY

The names that the author gives the fish are in many instances
the European common names. Where the common American
name is different, it is given in parenthesis immediately following the main entry.

FISHES

ANGELFISH: (Horned Butterfly Fish) *Heniochus acuminatus*
 Linnaeus
ARROW PIKE: *See* Barracuda
BARRACUDA: Sphyraenidae family
BAYARD: (Pompano) *Trachinotus blochi* Lacépède
"BOOBYFISH": *Naso* species
BOXFISH: *Ostracion* species
BUTTERFLY FISH: Chaetodontidae family
CARANX: *See* Mackerel
EMPEROR FISH: (Emperor Angelfish) *Pomacanthus imperator*
 Bloch

FILEFISH: Monacanthidae family

FIREFISH: (Lion Fish) *Pterois volitans* Linnaeus

FROGFISH: (Naked Scorpion Fish) Tetraroginae subfamily (of family Scorpaenidae)

GOLD DOTS: *Plectorhynchus* species

GOLDEN PERCH: (Golden Snapper) *Lutianus* species

GROUPER (serrated): *Epinephelus* species

HALAVI: (Guitar Fish) *Rhinobatus halavi* Forskål

HAMMERHEAD SHARK: *Sphyrna zygaena* Linnaeus

HARLEQUIN FISH: (Sea Dragon) *Phyllopteryx* species

JEWFISH: *Promicrops lanceolatus* Bloch

MACKEREL: (Jacks) *Caranx* species

MACKEREL SCAD: *Decapterus lajang* Bleeker

MAILED CHEEKS: Cataphracti order (includes scorpion fish, firefish, and *Synanceja*)

MANTA: *Manta birostris* Walbaum

MORAY EEL: Muraenidae family

PANTHER RAY: (Spotted-Eagle Ray) *Aetobatus narinari* Euphrasen

PARROT FISH: Scaridae family

PILOT FISH: *Naucrates ductor* Linnaeus

PIPEFISH: *Syngnathus* species

POMACENTRIDS: (Damselfishes) Pomacentridae family

POMPANO: *See* Bayard

PORCUPINE FISH: *Diodon hysterix* Linnaeus

PORPOISE: (Small Whales) Delphinidae family

"PUFFO": (Puffer Fish). *See* Sea Hedgehog

RHINOCEROS FISH: (Unicorn Fish) *Naso unicornis* Forskål

SAILFISH: *Istiophorus gladius* Broussonet

SAWFISH: Pristidae family

SEA HEDGEHOG: (Puffer or Globe Fish) *Tetraodon* species

SEA HORSE: *Hippocampus* species

SEA JUMPER: (Skipper or Rockhopper) Salariidae family

SHARKS: *Eulamia, Carcharias,* and *Carcharodon* species

SHEPHERD FISH: Stromateidae family

SNAPPER: Lutianidae family

SNIPEFISH: (Bird Fish or Bird Wrasse) *Gomphosus* species
SPINY-RAYED PERCH: Serranidae family
SQUIRREL FISH: Holocentridae family
SUCKING FISH: (Shark Sucker or Remora) *Echeneis naucrates*
    Linnaeus
SURGEONFISH: (Tangs) Acanthuridae family
SYNANCEJA: (Stone Fish). *See* Mailed Cheeks
TRIGGERFISH: Balistidae family

CORALS

ALCYONARIA: Octocorallia class
BRAIN CORAL: Meandrina genus
CATKINS: *Ammothea* species
COENOPSAMMIA: Eupsammiidae family
CROWN CORAL: *Madrepora* species
CUP-STAR CORAL: *Poecilopora* species
DERMOID ALCYONARIA: *Sympodium* species
FIRE CORAL: *Millepora* species
LACEWORK CORAL: *Porites* species
LEATHER CORAL: *See* Alcyonaria
MADREPORA: *See* Crown Coral
MEANDRINA: *See* Brain Coral
MONTIPORA: Montipora genus
MUSHROOM CORAL: *Fungia* species
ORGAN-PIPE CORAL: *Tubipora* species
PEN CORAL: *Stylophora* species
PRICKLY ALCYONARIA: *Spongodes* species
SEA WHIPS: Gorgonidae family
STAR CORAL: Astraeidae family
STINGING CORAL: *See* Fire Coral
THISTLE CORAL: *Seriatopora* species
XENIA CORAL: Xenia genus

INVERTEBRATES
OTHER THAN CORAL

CEPHALOPODA: Mollusca phylum

CUTTLEFISH: *See* Cephalopoda

JELLYFISH: Coelenterata phylum

MEDUSA: *See* Jellyfish

SALPA: Tunicata class. (This is not an invertebrate; it belongs to the Chordata phylum, but has no vertebra.)

SEA CUCUMBERS: Echinodermata, Holothuroidea class

SNAKE STARS: (Brittle Stars) Echinodermata, Ophiuroidea class

STARFISH: Echinodermata, Asteroidea class

Printed in the U.S.A.